The Best of Scanfest

An Authentic Treasury of Scandinavian Recipes and Proverbs

Edited by Cheryl Long

Culinary Arts Ltd.

Cover design and art by Bennett Stein
Interior art by Gun-Marie Rosqvist and Gorel Kinersly
Editorial Assistant - Jill Stanford Warren

Finnish proverbs used with permission from Finnish Proverbs,
translated by Inkeri Väänänen-Jensen. Published by Penfield Press
215 Brown St., Iowa City, Iowa 52245

Library of Congress Catalog Card Number: 91-059001

ISBN 0-914667-08-13

Printed in the United States of America

Published by:
Culinary Arts Ltd., P.O. Box 2157, Lake Oswego, Oregon 97035
In cooperation with The Scandinavian Heritage Foundation, Portland,
Oregon.

Books by Culinary Arts Ltd.:

Gourmet Vinegars: How To Make And Cook With Them
Gourmet Mustards: How To Make And Cook With Them
Easy Microwave Preserving
Classic Liqueurs: The Art Of Making And Cooking
                    With Liqueurs
The Best Of Scanfest: A Treasury of Authentic Recipes
                    and Proverbs

Publishers catalog available upon request

TABLE OF CONTENTS

PREFACE

This delightful innovative cookbook is one of several projects of the Scandinavian Heritage Foundation of Portland, Oregon planned to raise funds for the Scandinavian Studies Program at Portland State University and to build a permanent Scandinavian Cultural Center.

Since 1976, under the term, "Scandinavian Cluster," Portland State University has given courses in several Nordic languages. Support is sought to insure the continuance of these courses by contributing funds and eventually endowing a chair in Scandinavian studies.

By purchasing this book you are contributing to the continuation of a culture shared by a large number of citizens across this nation. With the building of the Scandinavian Cultural Center in Portland, Oregon and supporting the Scandinavian programs at Portland State University local Scandinavians are endeavoring to keep their heritage alive.

ACKNOWLEDGEMENTS

Sincere thanks to the many friends who have contributed time, translations, recipes and worked to assist in the compilation of this book. The following are noted for exceptional assistance:

Wenche Amlie, Astrid Jacobsen Ball, Aase Besson, Christine Brass, Ragnhild Bruun, Alan Chmura, Eila Sarvanto Chisholm, Gunvor Dahl, Marinne Eddington, Turid Q. Eide, Helen Ekeberg, Saara Slossar, G. Bernhard Fedde, Johanna Fedde, Lili Gregerson, Myrthle Griffin, Elsa Hansen, Bente Wiggins, Jan Johnson, Liisa Jyrkinen, Grethe Kasch, Ina Keski, Gorel Kinersly, Ron Kipp, Olaug Kremer, Lilly Kukkola, Kaino Leethem, Edith Lew, June Lofgren, Britt-Marie Lord, Ingeborg MacHaffie, Helga Magnusson, Svala Jonsdottir Mambert, Lisa Mendenhall, Martva Messer, Ellinor Mikkelsen, Inger Olsen, Carol O'Neil, June Pihl, Mel Pihl, Maj Persson, Elsie Rinta, Gun-Marie Rosqvist, Almira Sadevic, Jeffra Schultz-Andersen, Kaja Voldbæk, and Edda Vreed.

INTRODUCTION

The Scandinavians have developed a cuisine entirely their own - imaginative, colorful, and delicious, and served with creative elegance. Even in America, any food said to be Scandinavian bears the stamp of quality. The table is always beautiful, bountiful, and inviting - decorated with flowers, candles, and fancifully folded napkins.

There is an art to Scandinavian cooking. The best of ingredients are used, and the uniqueness comes in the combining of them. Notice the sauces, for instance, in which traditionally cream is used instead of milk.

Common to all the Scandinavian countries is the famous smørgäsbord. Adopted in America, the term is often applied to an assortment of potluck dishes, quite different from its original character. The Smörgåsbord is noted for its colorful array of appetizers, savory hot and cold dishes, salads, national cheeses, and ending with fancy desserts and delicate pastries.

The climate, extensive seacoasts, and proximity of the countries one to the other, as well as the history and nature of the peoples, have contributed to a number of similarities in food preparations and specialties. Take the herring, for example, which is prepared in many different ways and is invariably found as an appetizer along with other delectable tid-bits in all five countries.

Even though all Scandinavian cooking has aspects of similarity, each country is known for its own unusual fare, specialty, or national dish, reflecting its distinctive products and peoples. The following recipes have been collected from a number of knowledgeable and skilled Scandinavian cooks. They have been adapted and designed for American cooks to prepare, serve, and enjoy with Scandinavian taste and flair.

Ingeborg Nielsen MacHaffie
Author of <u>Of Danish Ways</u>

DENMARK

DENMARK

"Vær så god" or "Be so kind" (as to come to the table) is an invitation to eat, whether it is to an elaborate dinner (middag), served in the evening, or for lunch (frokost), the noon meal, which may consist of Smørrebrød, the renowned open-faced Danish sandwiches. You will not want to miss these intriguing and tempting concoctions, truly a connoisseur's delight, made from any number of various delectable ingredients and served with akvavit and/or genuine Danish beer.

Danish open-faced sandwiches are legendary. They are artistic and edible works of art which may be served alone or as part of a Smørrebrød. Try the Leverpostej (liver paste), a traditional sandwich spread; sliced Rullepølse (rolled and pressed spiced veal or pork). Ah, and don't forget the sweet-sour red cabbage — a must on any Danish menu. Then sample some of the cheeses, all made from the pure dairy products of Denmark — Danish blue cheese, Thybo, Danbo or Havarti.

The cold buffet may be followed by the main meal with hot entrees, or it may be the whole meal itself. For dinner, you may have Frikadeller (Danish meat patties) or pork tenderloin, often accompanied by the popular small, whole, sugar-glazed potatoes. Danes love potatoes — and gravy — and often you will see them in various forms at the same meal.

Take your pick from a multitude of fabulous desserts, which may range from puddings to pancakes. Some essential desserts to taste are: Danish Rødgrød, (a fresh berry pudding topped with light cream), Æblekage, (apple cake), or Æbleskiver (pancake balls). Almond paste is used in many Danish pastries. The Kransekage, a traditional wedding cake, is among your choices, and made entirely of almond paste.

Whether you have enjoyed a whole meal or merely an afternoon cup of coffee with layer cake and pastries, of course, you will say, "Tak for Mad!" (Thanks for the food!) or "Tak for Kaffe! (Thanks for the coffee!), and your hostess will respond with "Velbekomme!"

KIRSEBÆRLIKØR - CHERRY LIQUEUR

*This recipe is exceptionally close to the classic ruby-red Cherry Heering Liqueur from Denmark. Use dark Bing, or other sweet red cherries for the best flavor and color. You may vary the "almondish" taste by how you handle the cherry pits (see variation). Easy to make. Ready in 3 months. Makes about 1 quart. This recipe is used with permission from the cookbook, **CLASSIC LIQUEURS, The Art of Making and Cooking with Liqueurs** by Cheryl Long and Heather Kibbey.*

1½ lbs. red cherries, with pits, no stems
1½ to 2 cups granulated sugar (sweetness to taste)
2½ cups vodka
1 cup brandy

Mix vodka, brandy and sugar in a large glass measure or medium mixing bowl. Stir well to dissolve. Cut each washed cherry slightly to open, leave in pits. Place cherries in 2 sterile, quart wide mouth jars or 1 larger aging container. Pour liquid mixture over cherries, stir and cap with tight lids. For the first two weeks, stir mixture several times. Let age in a cool, dark place. Age 3 months, minimum, for best flavor. Strain off liqueur through wire mesh strainer, discard cherries. Strain again if needed for clarity. Re-bottle as desired.

Variation: ALMOND-CHERRY LIQUEUR - for a more prominent "almond" flavor, pit all or part of the cherries. Place cherry pits in a clean cloth and hit with a hammer to break them up slightly. Put broken pits and pitted cherries in jars or large container and continue as directed.

Variation: SUGARLESS CHERRY LIQUEUR - substitute 1 cup (8 oz.) apple juice concentrate, undiluted for the 1½ to 2 cups of sugar in this recipe. Proceed as directed. The "sugars" present will be natural fruit sugars rather than the granulated processed sugars. Taste is excellent; aging is the same.

RUGBRØD - RYEBREAD

This is the bread used for Danish open-faced sandwiches. In Denmark,
"no lunch is complete without ryebread".

2 packages yeast (use fresh yeast)
½ cup warm water
3 cups buttermilk
6 cups coarse rye flour
2 cups all-purpose flour
3 tsp. salt
2 to 4 tsp. Kitchen Bouquet (optional, to make the bread darker)
1 egg or egg white, optional for glaze

Dissolve yeast in warm water. Heat buttermilk slowly to lukewarm.
Add yeast to buttermilk, together with salt and Kitchen Bouquet, in
large mixing bowl. Add rye flour a little at a time, kneading well with
a spoon (or use dough hook on an electric mixer), until dough is firm
enough to knead with hands. Knead in the white flour with hands.
You may not need all the flour, the dough should be firm and moist,
but not sticky. Place dough in greased bowl and let rise in warm place
until double, about 45 minutes. Cover with a damp, clean cloth.

When double in size, turn onto lightly floured kitchen table and knead
again, lightly. Form into two loaves and place in greased loaf pans.
Rise again to double size. Prick the loaves with a fork, brush with egg
or egg white.

Bake in preheated oven at 400° F, about 45 to 50 minutes.

Giv ikke bagerens børn brød.

Don't give bread to the baker's children.

ÆBLESKIVER
APPLEDUMPLINGS OR PANCAKE BALLS

In Denmark, it is popular to serve Æbleskiver with hot wine or punch after dancing and singing around a huge bonfire on the eve of St. Hans, June 24th, the longest day of the year. This celebration dates back to the Dark Ages. It is usually served as a dessert or coffee pastry. Makes about 2 dozen.

1/3 cup butter or margarine
1 Tbsp. sugar
3 eggs
1½ cups milk
2 cups all-purpose flour
3 tsp. baking powder
1 tsp. lemon peel or grated lemon rind
2 tsp. ground cardamom

Whip softened butter and sugar, add eggs and beat well. Add flour, baking powder, cardamom, and rind, alternating with milk, a little at a time. Mix well. Fry in a special æbleskiverpan*.

Heat the pan and melt a little shortening in the bottom of the small cups. Fill the cups with dough about two-thirds full. Bake for a few minutes, turn the Æbleskiver with a fork or a knitting needle (it works well) and bake the other side. Keep turning the Æbleskiver around, until golden brown. It may take a little practice. Serve hot with powdered sugar, granulated sugar, and jam.

***Note**: Æbleskiverpans are usually found in Scandinavian import or cooking stores.

KRANSEKAGE - ALMOND WREATH

The wedding cake of Denmark can also be served at other celebrations.
When served at a wedding, a bride and groom top the cake. It is often
decorated with "knallerter" (paper crackers) and flags. Kransekage rings
are available in Scandinavian import or cooking stores.

3 lbs. canned almond paste
4 egg whites (½ cup) at room temperature
1 lb. powdered sugar

In a large saucepan, pick almond paste into smaller pieces and mix
with egg whites until blended. Heat over low heat (or in double
boiler) for 2 - 3 minutes, or until lukewarm and smooth, kneading all
the time, using a spoon or your hands. While heating, add as much
powdered sugar as the mixture will absorb; usually a full pound.

Oil ring molds with vegetable oil. Put mixture in a cookie press (use
the end that is used for cream puffs) or roll into finger-thick sausages.
Fit the dough into the rings and press ends together. With your
fingertips, press the almond rings together on top to form a ridge.
Bake in preheated oven on the lower shelf at 410° F for 8 to 10
minutes or until lightly golden. (Should be soft inside.)

Butter Icing:

1 egg white
2/3 cup powdered sugar
1 tsp. white distilled vinegar

Stir egg white with powdered sugar and vinegar until elastic and shiny,
approximately 10 minutes. With butter icing, make zigzag lines
around each ring, from outside to inside, starting with the largest ring.
Set the next largest ring on top of the first, and make the zigzag lines
around this ring, from outside to inside — in one continuous zigzag.
Repeat this process with each of the rings.

WIENERBRØD - DANISH PASTRY

This classic pastry of Denmark can be made in several variations. All of them will melt-in-your-mouth!

2 packages yeast (fresh preferred)
2/3 cup cold milk
1 egg
3 Tbsp. sugar
2 to 2½ cups all-purpose flour
2/3 to 1 cup cold butter or margarine

Dissolve yeast in cold milk. Whip egg and sugar slightly. Add to the yeast-milk mixture.

Stir in as much flour as needed to form a soft dough, then knead in more flour, until dough is smooth and elastic, but not too stiff or dry. Save remainder of flour to use for rolling out the dough.

Let the dough rest for about 15 minutes in the refrigerator, then roll out dough into a rectangular shape, as thin as possible (about one-eigth inch).

Cut the butter in thin slices and cover half of the dough with the slices. Fold the other half over the butter and roll into a rectangular shape. Then fold dough in thirds, give half a turn and roll again into rectangular shape. Repeat this folding in thirds, turning, and rolling another 2 to 3 times. If the dough gets too warm, put it back in the refrigerator until chilled, or else the dough gets sticky and difficult to handle. The quicker the rolling, the better the result. It is important to get the layered effect of dough and butter so the pastry is flaky when baked. Roll out the dough in a very thin, oblong shape. It is now ready for the filling.

Pastry Filling:

½ cup butter or margarine
½ cup granulated sugar
finely ground almonds
½ cup fine bread crumbs
almond flavoring to taste
½ cup raisins
1 egg or egg white
coarse pearl sugar

Soften butter and whip with granulated sugar. Add finely ground almonds, fine bread crumbs and almond flavoring to taste. Place filling in the middle of the dough, sprinkle with raisins, then fold the oblong edges of the dough toward center, press ends together so filling does not run out. Let rise for 20-30 minutes in shallow pan. Brush with egg or egg white, sprinkle with pearl sugar and chopped almonds. Bake 20-30 minutes in 400° F oven on middle shelf.

Variation: CARDAMOM FILLING - Soften ½ cup butter, whip with ½ to 1 cup sugar, add 1 tsp. ground cardamom. Spread with filling, sprinkle with cinnamon and raisens. Proceed as above.

Variation: CREAM AND JAM FILLING - Bring to boil ½ cup milk or light cream. Whip together 1 egg, 1 egg yolk, 3 tsps. cornstarch, 3 - 4 Tbsps. sugar, 2 tsps. vanilla. Add the boiling milk to the sugar-egg mixture, while still whipping. Pour back into casserole and bring to boil. Cool. Use this filling with different kinds of berry jams. Spread in middle of the dough; proceed as above.

Variation: SPANDAUERS - (small, individual "Danish") - Cut the dough in squares, place filling and jam in the middle. Sprinkle dough with cardamom, fold tips of squares toward the middle. Let rise for 20 - 30 minutes, brush with egg, and bake as described above. Cool before frosting. Frost with a white frosting made from powdered sugar stirred with egg white. Sprinkle with slivered almonds.

FRANSKE VAFLER - FRENCH WAFERS

A pastry confection always found in Danish bakeries. Makes 20 wafers.

Wafers:

2 cups all-purpose flour
1 cup (2 sticks) butter or margarine, softened
1/3 cup water

Prepare dough by cutting butter into flour with a pastry cutter or in a food processor. Gradually add the water. Once the dough is smooth, let it rest in refrigerator for at least one hour. Roll dough with a regular rolling pin until it is thin, yet not too thin to be rolled further. Cut dough into round pieces with a small glass. Roll each individual round piece lightly in sugar with a textured rolling pin, until it takes an oval shape. Make sure it is rolled until sugar is absorbed on both sides. Bake on greased baking sheet in a 325° F oven, about 12 minutes, until sugar coating melts and makes the wafers light brown. Put two wafers together with cream filling in between.

Filling:

1/3 cup butter
1 cup powdered sugar
1 tsp. vanilla

Mix butter, powdered sugar, and vanilla. Whip until fluffy. Put the wafers together with this filling.

Øvelse gør mester. - Practice makes perfect.

LAGKAGE - LAYER CAKE

A recipe prepared with "old country" measurements. Try it for fun, you'll try it again for taste!

Fill 3 equal-sized glasses with:

4 eggs in first glass
sugar to same height in second glass
all-purpose flour to same height in third glass
2 tsp. baking powder

Grease three 9" cake pans (preferably with loose bottoms). Sprinkle with bread crumbs.

Whip eggs and sugar until thick and lemon-colored. Fold in flour and baking powder. Blend quickly. Pour batter into prepared pans. Bake in preheated oven at 375° F for 6 to 8 minutes. Cool on rack.

Spread bottom layer with a custard filling*. Cover with second layer and spread with berry jam, such as strawberry, raspberry, or boysenberry jam, or lightly sweetened fresh fruits. Cover with third layer. Mix powdered sugar with a little hot water or egg whites for frosting.

Serve with whipped cream on the side or decorate the cake with the whipped cream just before serving. The layer cake is best when put together several hours before serving so the fruit fillings have time to blend with the cake.

*Note: For vanilla custard, see filling for orange trifle or make instant vanilla pie filling whipped with light cream or whipping cream.

GAMMELDAGS ÆBLEKAGE
OLD-FASHIONED APPLECAKE

Traditionally served on St. Martin's Day, (November 11th), in Denmark and Sweden. Instead of fresh apples, a good, thick canned applesauce may be substituted in this recipe.

2 lbs. apples (Granny Smith are excellent)
grated rind of ½ lemon
sugar to taste
vanilla to taste
½ cup butter or margarine
2 cups bread crumbs
1 cup sugar

Garnish:

whipped, sweetened cream
currant or red jelly

Peel and core apples, cut in thin slices. Cook apples and lemon rind in a saucepan with as little water as possible, just enough to prevent scorching. Cook until apples are tender, and mash them as for applesauce.

Add sugar and vanilla to taste. Do not sweeten too much, the applesauce should be a little on the tart side. Cool.

Melt butter in a skillet to a golden brown, add bread crumbs and sugar. Toast, while you keep stirring, so the crumbs do not scorch. When the bread crumbs have turned nicely golden, remove skillet from heat and let the mixture cool while you stir occasionally. Put a thin layer of the cooled bread crumbs in a deep bowl, then a layer of the cooled applesauce, continue layering until the bowl is filled, ending with the bread crumbs. (Do the layering about 1 hour before serving.)

Serve with whipped cream. You may also, before serving, decorate the applecake with the whipped cream and dots of red currant jelly (or other kinds of red jelly).

Variation: ALMOND APPLECAKE - Layer applesauce with crushed almond macaroons, layered as above, beginning and ending with the macaroons. Serve with whipped cream.

Variation: RED CURRANT APPLECAKE - Layer thinly bread crumbs, applesauce, red currant jelly, alternating as above, beginning and ending with the bread crumbs. Serve with whipped cream.

VANILLEKRANSE - VANILLA WREATH COOKIES

A Christmas in Denmark is not a real Christmas without these cookies. Makes about 6 dozen.

4 cups all-purpose flour
2/3 cup sugar
12/3 cups butter or margarine
4 oz. blanched almonds, finely chopped
1 egg
1 vanilla bean, finely chopped, or 2 tsp. vanilla flavoring
¼ tsp. baker's ammonia

Knead together flour, baker's ammonia, butter, sugar, egg, and vanilla. Knead well, the dough should be smooth. Choose a star pattern for the cookie press, fill the press, form rings on greased cookie sheets, bake until golden brown in 325° to 350° F oven. Store in airtight containers.

KÆRNEMÆLKSSUPPE
BUTTERMILK SOUP, COLD

A favorite dessert in the summertime that is served cold, topped with crushed corn flakes and/or chopped almonds. Serves 6.

2 eggs, separated
6 cups buttermilk
½ to 2/3 cup sugar
vanilla and lemon rind to taste

Whip the egg whites until stiff, set aside. Whip the egg yolks and sugar together until thick and lemony. Add the buttermilk and the flavoring to the egg yolk and sugar mixture. Fold the stiff-beaten egg whites into the buttermilk-egg mixture just before serving.

Man kan ikke få både i pose og i sæk.

You cannot have it both ways.

KÆRNEMÆLKSSUPPE
BUTTERMILK SOUP, WARM

Traditionally served before the main course with sliced or chopped almonds, or with whipped cream and strawberry, raspberry, or blackberry jam. If served with jam, omit raisins. In some regions it is served after the main course. Serves 6.

3 Tbsp. all-purpose flour
6 cups buttermilk
½ cup raisins or berry jam
lemon rind, cinnamon stick
2 to 3 eggs
½ cup sugar

Mix the flour with a little of the buttermilk to make a thin paste. Slowly add the rest of the buttermilk and the other ingredients, except eggs and sugar. Heat over medium heat, very slowly, whipping constantly, so the buttermilk does not curdle.

Whip eggs and sugar in a big bowl, until thick and lemony. When the soup reaches boiling point, remove from heat and add to the bowl with the egg-sugar mixture, while whipping. Serve at once, warm.

APPELSINTRIFLI - ORANGE TRIFLE

The Danish version of a "trifle".

4 oranges
8 to 10 large almond macaroons
4 Tbsp. Madeira, sherry or rum

Garnish:

whipped, sweetened cream
grated chocolate
chopped filberts
reserved orange slices

Vanilla Cream:

2 egg yolks
4 Tbsp. sugar
2 tsp. all-purpose flour
vanilla to taste
1 cup milk or half and half
1/3 cup whipping cream, whipped

Make the vanilla cream first: Whip the egg yolks with sugar and flour, add the milk and vanilla. Bring to a boil in a saucepan over medium heat, whipping constantly. Be careful that the cream does not scorch. When mixture comes to a full boil, time for 1 minute or more. Cool, stirring occasionally. When completely cool, add whipped cream.

Peel the oranges, cut in thin slices, then divide them into smaller pieces. Set aside a few slices for garnish. In a deep bowl, place 2 or 3 almond macaroons in the bottom, sprinkle with some of the wine. Now add a layer of vanilla cream, then a layer of orange slices. Repeat these layers until bowl is filled, ending with the macaroons.

Before serving, decorate the trifle with a layer of whipped cream, sprinkle with grated chocolate and chopped filberts, garnish with orange slices.

Variation: **ABRIKOSTRIFLI - APRICOT TRIFLE** - Substitute 8 ounces of dried apricots for oranges. Cover apricots with 2 cups of water. Soak for 24 hours. Cook apricots in soaking water, stirring often, until tender and water is evaporated. Be careful not to scorch apricot mixture. Apricots will be mushy, beat to a thick, sauce-like consistancy. Add 1 cup sugar, cool, then layer as above.

Tip: An instant vanilla pie filling or cooked vanilla pie filling may be used instead of the vanilla cream.

RIS Á L'AMANDE - RICE DESSERT

Serve with a lukewarm fruit sauce, preferably dark cherries. This is a traditional Danish Christmas dessert. Before serving, one whole blanched almond is added to the pudding, and the lucky person who finds the almond in his serving receives a gift. The custom is to give a little pig made of almond paste with a red ribbon tied around its neck. Serves 4.

1 whole vanilla bean or 2 tsp. vanilla extract
2 cups milk or half and half
½ cup pearl rice
3 Tbsp. sugar
2 oz. blanched almonds, chopped
1/3 cup whipping cream, whipped
1 whole almond

Continued next page

Cut the vanilla bean open and scrape out the seeds. Add both bean and seeds to the milk. Bring the milk to a boil in a saucepan over medium heat, and add the rice. Bring back to boil, reduce the heat and let the rice simmer for approximately 25 to 30 minutes. Do not cover the pan. When rice is tender, add sugar and vanilla flavoring, if you do not use the vanilla bean. Cool, while stirring occasionally. Remove vanilla bean. Add almonds to the cold rice pudding, together with the whipped cream. Whip well, until the pudding is light and fluffy. Stir in one whole almond if desired.

QUICK CHERRY SAUCE: Heat 1 can (15 oz.) dark, sweet cherry pie filling and ¼ to ½ tsp. almond extract, to taste and serve.

RØDGRØD MED FLØDE
RED FRUIT PUDDING WITH CREAM

Rødgrød is the Danes national dessert. Best made from various fruits such as: equal parts of currants and raspberries, currants and black currants, currants and cherries, or strawberries and currants. Rhubarb is the most common fruit that is used to make this dessert. Serves 4 to 6.

1½ lbs. berries or fruit
¾ liter water (3 cups)
½ cup sugar
2 Tbsp. cornstarch or potato starch*

Clean the berries, boil them in water until tender. Strain. Pour juice back into casserole and bring back to boil. Sweeten and thicken with cornstarch dissolved in a little cold water. Boil until pudding jells. Cool in bowl, sprinkled with a little sugar to avoid skin on pudding.

*Note: If using potato starch dissolved in a little cold water, do not boil after potato starch is added to the sweetened, boiling juice. To do so will make the pudding rubbery.

CITRONFROMAGE - LEMON FLUFF

A light and lovely dessert. Decorate with whipped cream, sprinkled with chopped nuts, grated chocolate, or mandarin oranges. Serves 6 to 8.

8 eggs, separated
1 cup sugar
2 Tbsp. gelatin
¼ cup cold water
½ cup boiling water
½ cup lemon juice
1 Tbsp. grated lemon rind

Garnish:

whipped, sweetened cream
chopped nuts
grated chocolate
mandarin oranges

Beat eggs yolks with sugar until thick and lemon colored. Soften gelatin in a little cold water and add ½ cup of boiling water. Stir until dissolved. Add lemon juice and grated lemon rind to the gelatin mixture, then add the lemon-gelatin mixture to the whipped egg yolks. Cool until the mixture begins to jell*, then carefully fold in stiffly beaten egg whites. Pour into a glass serving bowl or individual dessert bowls. Keep cool until serving.

*Tip: To hasten the jelling process, set the bowl with the gelatin-egg yolk mixture in cold water and stir off and on.

SVIGERMORS ORANGE MARMALADE
MOTHER-IN-LAW'S ORANGE MARMALADE

Makes about 8 to 10 pints.

3 lbs. oranges (thin-skinned)
1 lemon
1 lb. apricots, fresh or dried*
6 cups water
2 lbs. sugar for each 4 cups fruit pulp

Grind the oranges, lemon and apricots through a meat grinder. Soak overnight in six cups water.

Next day, bring fruit mixture and water to boil in large kettle, without sugar, reduce heat and simmer for 1½ to 2 hours. Remove from heat.

Measure fruit: For each 4 cups of the fruit pulp, add 2 pounds sugar. Return to boil, stir often to be sure the marmalade does not scorch. Simmer for ½ hour or until marmalade becomes jelled (glassy). Pour into sterilized jars and seal immediately.

Note: Dried apricots give more flavor.

Selvgjort er velgjort.

What you can do yourself is the best.

FRIKADELLER - DANISH MEAT BALLS

For luncheon parties, smaller frikadeller are common. To make them use a smaller spoon. Serve with pickled beets or sweet dill pickles. For dinner, a normal-sized tablespoon gives the right size for main meal patties. Serve with creamed peas and carrots, potatoes, or other vegetables. Serves 4.

½ lb. ground veal
½ lb. ground pork
3 to 4 Tbsp. all-purpose flour
½ cup grated onion
2 eggs
salt and pepper to taste
1½ to 2 cups milk
butter or margarine for frying

Combine meats, flour, onion, eggs, and spices in a deep mixing bowl. Add milk, little by little, while beating or whipping with an electric mixer, mix well. Let the mixture rest for about 15 to 30 minutes in refrigerator. In a skillet, melt butter over medium heat. With a tablespoon, form oval meat patties and drop into the skillet. Let brown on one side, then turn patties to brown on the other side until done in the center, about 4 minutes on each side.

Note: To form the patties: Dip the tablespoon in melted butter, push the meat mixture against one side of the bowl, carve out enough meat dough to form an oblong shape with the spoon before dropping it into the skillet. The "Frikadelle" gets its oblong shape from the spoon used.

Græd ikke over spildt mælk. - Don't cry over spilled milk.

BEDSTEMORS LÆKRE LEVERPOSTEJ
GRANDMOTHER'S DELICIOUS LIVERPASTE

A lean liverpaste that uses a different meat base than the traditional one.

1 lb. chicken liver
1 lb. ground pork
1 medium onion
6 anchovies
½ cup all-purpose flour
1 to 1¼ cups cream or milk
3 eggs
¼ tsp. each cloves and allspice
salt and pepper to taste

Chop chicken liver, pork, onion and anchovies in a food processor or meat grinder 4 to 5 times. Add rest of ingredients to the liver mixture, stir well. Pour batter into a loaf pan. Set loaf pan in a larger pan of hot water. Bake 1 hour, or until done in a 350° F oven. Remove baked loaf from pan when cool.

Kommer tid, kommer råd. - There will always be a way.

LEVERPOSTEJ - LIVERPASTE

A classic Scandinavian Liverpaste. Wonderful for open-faced sandwiches.

1½ lbs. calf or pork liver
3 slices French bread
2/3 cup milk
9 slices bacon
4 onions, small
5 to 6 anchovies
2/3 cup (at least) cream
3 eggs
pinch pepper, allspice, and timian
½ Tbsp. all-purpose flour
1 tsp. salt

Chop the liver finely. Soak bread in milk. Add soaked bread, 6 strips of bacon, onions, and anchovies to liver and chop (in a food processor or meat grinder). Add remaining ingredients, including at least two-thirds cup cream. Grind through the meat grinder 3 or 4 times (or food processor) to get a smooth paste. Pour the soft batter in a large loaf pan. Cover with 3 strips of bacon cut in half. Set loaf pan in a larger pan of hot water. Bake 1 hour, or until done in a 350° F oven. Remove baked loaf from pan when cool.

Man kan ikke gøre alle tilpas.

You cannot please everybody.

KALVERULLEPØLSE - ROLLED VEAL SAUSAGE

This meat is delicious on ryebread, open-faced, decorated with Remoulade or Italian Salad. The sausage is traditionally cut in fairly thin slices.

1 thin piece breast of veal (ask butcher to remove the breast bones and trim)

Spice Mixture:

½ to 1 tsp. pepper
1 tsp. salt
1 medium onion, chopped
½ tsp. allspice
½ tsp. saltpeter, optional

Trim the meat to a rectangular shape. Rub with salt and a little saltpeter. Place the meat with the side up from which the bones were removed. Sprinkle with the spice mixture. (If the breast of veal is too lean, add very thin slices of pork fat trimmings, layered in the entire length of the meat.) Roll the veal tightly from the shortest side of the rectangle to form a sausage. Stick a fork in the middle to hold sausage together while sewing the three sides together with a thin, strong cotton string. Then tie the sausage, just like the butchers do with boneless roasts, its entire length.

Put the sausage in a cold brine for 3-4 days.

Brine:

2 quarts water
1¼ cup salt
½ tsp. saltpeter, optional
1/3 cup brown sugar

Mix spices with the water, bring to a boil. Cool, then add sausage.
You may have to put slight pressure on the sausage to keep it
submerged (an inverted plate will do nicely). After 3 or 4 days the
sausage is ready to be boiled.

Fill a large kettle with cold water, enough to cover the sausage. Bring
to boil over medium heat. Simmer sausage for 35 to 40 minutes per
pound of sausage.

When sausage is cooked, remove immediately from the casserole and
put between two flat boards, and add weight to the top board in order
to press the sausage into a rectangular shape. Leave the sausage
overnight, or until cold, between the boards. The Danes use a special
device (Rullepølsepresser): 2 wooden boards with screws in each
corner which can be tightened to add the desired pressure on the
sausage and give the shape.

SVINEKOTELETTER MED SVAMPESTUVNING
PORK CHOPS WITH MUSHROOMS

A rich and memorable entree. Serves 4.

salt and pepper to taste
bread crumbs
1 egg
shortening or margarine for frying
4 thick pork chops, with or without bones

Mix salt and pepper with the bread crumbs. Whip egg lightly, turn the pork chops in egg, then in bread crumbs. Heat shortening in skillet, brown pork chops lightly on both sides, and place them in a shallow dish. Cook off the skillet with a little water (very little) and pour drippings over chops. Cover and bake in moderate oven, 325° to 350° F, about 45 minutes.

CREAMED MUSHROOMS

This may be made and served with many dishes but is given here to be poured over pork chops or served in a gravy boat alongside.

8 to 10 oz. mushrooms
2 Tbsp. butter
1 to 11/3 cups heavy cream or undiluted evaporated milk
1 Tbsp. lemon
Kitchen Bouquet
salt and pepper to taste

Clean and slice mushrooms. (If small, leave whole or cut in halves.) Cook in skillet with butter until nicely browned and the moisture from the mushrooms has evaporated.

Pour heavy cream, lemon, and Kitchen Bouquet into skillet. Simmer with the mushrooms until the gravy is sufficiently thick and concentrated. Add salt and pepper to taste.

MØRBRAD MED ÆBLER OG SVESKER
PORK TENDERLOIN WITH APPLES AND PRUNES

A wonderful fall dish. Serve with potatoes and red cabbage. Serves 4.

1 to 2 pork tenderloins
3 small apples
12 to 14 prunes, pitted
salt, pepper and sugar to taste
butter or margarine for frying
boiling water or bouillon
heavy cream or half and half
Kitchen Bouquet

Cut each of the tenderloins down the entire length, almost all the way through, and open the meat up so you have two almost flat pieces. Then place the peeled, sliced apples, softened prunes, a little salt and sugar on one of the pieces, place the other tenderloin on top of the filling, and fasten the edges with toothpicks. If you only have one tenderloin, fill half of the loin, then fold the other half over the filling. Fasten the edges.

Heat skillet with a little margarine and brown the tenderloin until golden on both sides. Sprinkle with salt and pepper, and add boiling water or bouillon (very little). Cover and braise for about ½ hour. Remove tenderloin from skillet. Add a little cream, butter, and Kitchen Bouquet to liquid in skillet and cook down until the gravy thickens.

Before serving, remove the toothpicks and cut in serving pieces. Pour some of the gravy over and serve the rest in a gravy boat.

HELLEFLYNDERKOTELETER MED PERSILLESOVS
HALIBUT CUTLETS WITH PARSLEY SAUCE

Serve with lemon, Remoulade, and small, boiled potatoes. Pickled beets are also served with fried fish in Denmark. Serves 4.

1 egg
2 lbs. halibut fillet, cut in serving pieces
1/3 to ½ cup fine bread crumbs
2 Tbsp. salt
½ tsp. white pepper
butter, margarine or oil, for frying

Beat egg lightly. Turn the pieces of fish in egg, then in the bread crumbs, sprinkle with salt and pepper. Heat butter in skillet. Fry the fish until firm and golden brown on both sides.

Parsley Sauce for Fish:

¼ cup butter or margarine
4 to 5 Tbsp. all purpose flour
11/3 cups milk
salt to taste
chopped parsley

Melt butter in a saucepan, stir in flour until the paste is smooth. Add milk, a little at a time, until gravy has the right consistency. Add salt to taste. Before serving, add finely chopped parsley.

Variation: HALIBUT GRAVY - Add ¼ cup flour to drippings in pan, stir until smooth. Add milk, a little at a time, until the gravy has the consistency desired. Add salt to taste and if preferred, finely chopped parsley.

KRYDDERFEDT - APPLE-ONION LARD

This lard is used as a spread on open-faced sandwiches, especially with pickled herring, salami, liverpaste or corned beef. Also good on ryebread with cheeses, preferably Danish cheeses such as Havarti, Thybo or Tilsitter.

1 lb. lard
2 medium onions, thinly sliced or chopped
2 small apples, thinly sliced or chopped
1 tsp. each: thyme, salt, pepper

Melt lard slowly together with onions, apples and spices. Let simmer for about ½ hour to let lard absorb flavors. Cool, stirring often, then pour into stoneware container. Keep in refrigerator.

DYRLÆGENS NATMAD
THE VETERINARIAN'S NIGHTCAP

This classic open-face sandwich uses Apple-onion lard. Try it!

Ryebread with apple-onion lard
Thick slice of liverpaste
Covered with "Sky" (beef bouillon, with gelatin)
Topped with generous slices of corned beef

Æblet falder ikke langt fra stammen.

The apple does not fall far from the tree.

REMOULADE-RELISH

This seemingly simple relish is used on many foods in Denmark. An interesting variation adds chopped, cooked cauliflower. Excellent with seafood, sandwiches, meats, or as a garnish.

Simple recipe:

¼ cup hot dog relish
¼ cup sweet dill relish
1 cup mayonnaise
1 tsp. onion powder

Mix and serve as garnish. Store, covered, in refrigerator.

Traditional recipe:

1 cup mayonnaise
½ cup chopped, sweet dill pickles (or sweet dill relish)
3 to 4 tsp. curry
1 tsp. mustard powder
1 Tbsp. chopped onion
1 hard-boiled egg, chopped
dash garlic
capers, optional

Mix all ingredients. Store, covered, in refrigerator.

PEBERRODSSALAT - HORSERADISH WHIP

Outstanding served on ryebread with roast beef, sprinkled with crisp-fried onions. Horseradish Whip is also excellent with entrees, such as prime rib.

1 cup heavy cream, whipped with a teaspoon of sugar
2 to 3 tsp. prepared or creamed horseradish

Mix whipped cream and horseradish. Add more horseradish, if you like it nippy. Keep refrigerated.

VARM KARTOFFELSALAT - HOT POTATO SALAD

Traditionally served with wieners and many meat and fish dishes. Serves 4 to 6.

2 lbs. small, firm potatoes
1/3 cup butter or margarine
2 medium onions
¼ cup vinegar
¼ cup water
1 tsp. salt
½ tsp. pepper
2 Tbsp. sugar
half and half, optional

Cook potatoes, peel, cool, and cut in slices. Heat butter and add sliced onions, sauté until golden. Add vinegar, water, spices and sugar, stirring constantly. When the onions are tender, add the sliced potatoes. Heat, while still stirring, at medium setting. Add more sugar if not sweet enough. A little half and half may be added to give a richer taste.

SYLTEDE RØDBEDER - PICKLED BEETS

Decorates meat and fish dishes as well as open-faced sandwiches.

8 beets, large
2 cups distilled white vinegar
1 cup water
cinnamon stick
2 Tbsp. pickling spice

Wash beets and cook in water about 1 hour or until tender. Pour off hot beet water. Cover beets with cold water. When cooled slightly, peel beets and cut in thin slices. Place the beets in a jar. Mix vinegar, water, cinnamon stick and spices in a casserole. Bring to boil. Pour immediately over the beets in the jar. Vinegar mixture should cover the beets completely. Let stand for 24 hours before serving.

AGURKESALAT - CUCUMBER SALAD

Best when the cucumber has time to blend with vinegar and spices. Serve either with meat dishes or as a garnish on open-faced sandwiches.

1 English cucumber
salt

Dressing:

4 to 5 Tbsp. salad oil
2 Tbsp. white, distilled vinegar
1 Tbsp. each: water, sugar
salt and pepper to taste

Dissolve sugar in lukewarm water. Add oil, vinegar and seasonings. Wash, dry and peel cucumber. Slice very thin. Place the slices in a bowl. Sprinkle salt over cucumber slices, then add a light weight to the cucumber, and leave in a cool place for about an hour. Discard accumulated liquid. Rinse lightly, pat dry, and pour dressing over the cucumber slices. Keep in refrigerator.

ITALIENSK SALAT - ITALIAN SALAD

Serve as garnish with ham or veal sausage on open-faced sandwiches.

2 cups peas and carrots, cooked
3 heaping Tbsp. mayonnaise
1 heaping Tbsp. sour cream or heavy cream, whipped
1 tsp. lemon juice
dash garlic powder
dash paprika

Mix mayonnaise and drained peas and carrots. Add lemon juice. Add spices and toss. Fold in sour or whipped cream. Keep in refrigerator until ready to use.

Variation: ITALIAN SALAD WITH ASPARAGUS AND PASTA

Add ½ cup cooked miniature macaroni or ½ cup cooked, cut asparagus to the salad.

REJESALAT - SHRIMP SALAD

Serve in a bowl garnished with hard-boiled eggs and chives or sprigs of dill weed. May be served on slices of French bread.

1 lb. shrimp, cleaned and cooked
½ cup mayonnaise
salt and white pepper to taste
lemon juice to taste
½ cup heavy cream, whipped or sour cream, or a little of both
chopped chives or sprigs of dill weed for decoration
hard-boiled eggs for decoration

Mix together mayonnaise, whipped or sour cream, and seasonings. Toss shrimp with the mayonnaise/cream mixture. Add a little lemon if you use only the heavy cream.

Sæt tæring efter næring.

Use only as much as you can afford.

DANSK SMØRREBRØD
DANISH OPEN-FACED SANDWICHES

When Danes serve open-faced sandwiches for parties, pickled herring and/or warm plaice with Remoulade and lemon slices are always served first.

Usually served on Rugbrød* - Ryebread (also called Danish Pumpernickel)

Topping Suggestions:

Leverpostej* (Liverpaste) with crisp bacon and sauteed mushrooms or with red cabbage or cucumber salad, garnished with strips of jellied consomme.

Thin slices of pork roast with Rødkål* (red cabbage), apples, and prunes. Garnish with thin slices of orange (cut into middle of slice, then twist and put crosswise over the red cabbage).

Boiled tongue of veal with Italian Salad*. Garnish with thin tomato slices, same way as above.

Thin slices of Kalverullepølse* (rolled veal sausage) with Italian Salad* or Remoulade*. Garnish with thin slices of sweet onion and jellied consomme.

Thin slices of ham with Italian Salad* or Horseradish Whip*. Garnish with orange slices or tomato slices.

Slices of ham with scrambled egg, sprinkled with chives, garnished with tomato wedges.

Corned beef with Italian Salad* or Remoulade*, jellied consomme.

Thin slices of roast beef with Remoulade* or Horseradish Whip*, sprinkle with crisp fried onions, sweet dill pickles, cut and twisted across the salad sauce.

French Bread Topping Suggestions:

Rejesalat* (shrimp salad) with lemon slices and tomato wedges.

Fresh, smoked salmon with scrambled egg, sprinkled with chives.

Gravlax* (pickled salmon) with mustard sauce.

*Note: Recipes that are starred can be found in this cookbook.

HØNSEKØDSUPPE MED BOLLER
CHICKEN SOUP WITH DUMPLINGS

Chicken soup with dumplings is often served before entrees at big parties, such as weddings, anniversaries or confirmations. Special small meatballs and dumplings are usually added. Serves 4 to 6.

10 to 12 cups of cold water
1 large chicken
1 beef soup bone
3 large leeks, sliced
3 carrots, thinly sliced
1 parsnip, thinly sliced
6 stalks celery, sliced
salt to taste

Bring water to boil in a large kettle. Add the chicken and soup bone. Bring back to boil, remove any foam collecting on top of water. Simmer chicken and soup bone for an hour, then add the vegetables and salt. Simmer until all vegetables and chicken are tender.

Before serving, remove chicken and soup bone. Chicken may be deboned and cut up and returned to soup or served separately.

MELBOLLER - SOUP DUMPLINGS

Dumplings may be made ahead and warmed up in soup before serving, or added to soup after it is cooked. Makes about 5 dozen.

1 cup boiling water
½ cup butter or margarine
1 cup all-purpose flour
4 eggs
salt and sugar to taste

Bring water to boil, add butter, bring back to boil. Then add the flour while stirring vigorously with a spoon until the dough is smooth and shiny and leaves side of saucepan and spoon. Cool. Add eggs, one at a time, beating well. Add salt and a little sugar for taste.

Form small balls with a teaspoon and drop them, one by one, into boiling water. Cook for about 3-5 minutes. Be careful not to boil rapidly, but let the water stay on constant simmer. Cool in cold water.

Note: There is a special press used for making meat balls and dumplings. It may be available in Scandinavian speciality stores.

KØDBOLLER - MEAT BALLS FOR SOUP

Serve in a variety of soups or broths, either immediately; or, if made in advance, warmed in the soup. Makes about 4 dozen.

½ lb. ground lean pork
½ lb. ground lean veal
2 Tbsp. all-purpose flour
1 tsp. potato starch, or cornstarch
salt, pepper to taste
1 cup milk

Beat the meat together with the flour, starch, spices and milk, until the dough is well mixed and smooth. Let rest for an hour or so. Form small balls with a teaspoon and drop them, one by one, into boiling, lightly salted water. Boil for 4 to 5 minutes, until done. (The meat balls will drop to the bottom when added to the water and rise when they are done.) Avoid a rolling boil, rather, keep the water on a simmer.

Uden mad og drikke duer helten ikke.

Without food and drink, the hero is good for nothing.

CHAMPIGNONSUPPE
CREAM OF MUSHROOM SOUP

A rich soup that can star as a soup course or entree. Serves 4 to 6.

1 lb. mushrooms
½ cup (1 stick) butter or margarine
9 to 10 cups chicken broth
1 medium onion, chopped
2½ Tbsp. all-purpose flour
½ cup heavy whipping cream
salt and white pepper to taste
lemon juice and sherry to taste

Clean and rinse the mushrooms thoroughly. Dry lightly in paper towel. Chop or cut in thin slices, then sauté in butter until golden. Add the chopped onion and sauté for about 10 minutes, stirring often. Add to the broth in sauce pan, bring to boil.

Stir flour with water to a smooth paste and add the mixture to the boiling soup to thicken the soup slightly. Add cream and spices to taste, together with the lemon juice and sherry.

Det er bedre med een fugl i hånden, end ti på taget.

**You are better off with one bird in the hand
than ten on the roof.**

OKSEHALESUPPE - OXTAIL SOUP

For parties, it would be better to take the meat from the bones before serving, but otherwise, serve the soup just as it is. When served with ryebread, it makes a very nourishing main meal. Serves 4 to 6.

3 to 4 lbs. oxtails, cut into pieces
2 carrots, diced
1 medium onion, chopped
4 stalks celery, chopped
¼ cup margarine or shortening
salt and paprika to taste
6 to 8 cups cold water
sherry to taste

Sauté carrots, onion and celery in margarine or shortening until golden. Remove from pan, and brown the oxtails in the drippings. Put the oxtails, drippings and water in a large kettle, bring water to boil, and simmer for 3 to 4 hours, until the oxtails are tender.

Just before the oxtails are done, add the vegetables, and cook for about 20 minutes, or until done. Add salt and paprika to taste. Just before serving, add the sherry.

GRØNLANGKÅL FRA JYLLAND
CREAMED KALE FROM JUTLAND

*Kale is often traditionally served sprinkled with a sugar-
cinnamon mixture. Usually accompanied by pork or ham with mustard
for lunch on the day of Christmas Eve and all through the holidays for
family gatherings. Serves 4.*

1 lb. kale
water
salt and sugar to taste

Wash and rip kale from the stalks. Bring water to boil with salt and
sugar to taste in a large casserole. Add the kale and simmer for about
15 minutes. If using frozen kale, cook according to package
directions. When tender, remove from water, drain. Cool and chop
finely or put through meat grinder. Add kale to the white sauce.

WHITE SAUCE:

¼ cup butter or margarine
4 to 5 Tbsp. all purpose flour
11/3 cups milk
salt, to taste

Melt butter in casserole. Add flour and stir to form a smooth paste.
Add milk, little by little, until gravy thickens. Bring to a boil, stirring
constantly so the gravy does not scorch. If the gravy is too thick, add
more milk.

Variation: KALE BALLS FROM VENDSYSSEL - In the northern part of Denmark, kale is formed into small balls and then frozen for future use. Many pounds of kale are boiled in a rich soup, made of fresh side of pork, or lamb, or both. The kale boils for several hours, then is removed from the soup, drained, and then formed into balls. As you form the balls, all the liquid should be squeezed out with your hands.

When ready to serve, the balls are cut in smaller pieces and placed in a skillet with melted butter, heated slowly. Add light cream and heat. Serve kale sprinkled with sugar-cinnamon mixture. Serve cold meat alongside.

STUVEDE GRØNÆRTER OG GULERØDDER
CREAMED PEAS AND CARROTS

Served with meat dishes, such as Danish meat balls. The wonder of this dish is the "smørbolle". A handy idea for a number of creamed dishes. Serves 4 to 6.

2 (10 oz.) packages frozen peas and carrots
3 Tbsp. all-purpose flour
3 Tbsp. butter or margarine
salt to taste
dash sugar
finely chopped parsley

Boil the peas and carrots according to directions in enough boiling water to cover the vegetables. In a small bowl, mix butter with the flour until a smooth paste forms. It will be fairly thick, will look like a small butter ball. (A butter ball in Danish is called "smørbolle.") Add this butter ball to the boiling peas and carrots; it will thicken the sauce or gravy. If you don't think the gravy is thick enough, add a little more butter and flour. Add salt and sugar to taste. Just before serving, add finely chopped parsley to the peas and carrots.

RØDKÅL - RED CABBAGE

A Danish favorite among vegetables. It is served as a side dish and on many dishes and sandwiches.

1 large head red cabbage
½ cup sugar
¼ cup white distilled vinegar
½ cup currant jelly or currant juice
butter or margarine

Wash the cabbage head and remove the outer leaves. Cut into 4 parts, remove inner stalk. Chop or shred cabbage finely. Place in a large casserole. Add vinegar and simmer for approximately 1 hour, then add currant jelly or juice and sugar. Add more vinegar and/or sugar, if necessary. Also watch carefully that the cabbage does not scorch. Stir occasionally. Cook until tender. Add 2 tablespoons butter to the cabbage before serving to make the cabbage nice and shiny.

BRUNEDE KARTOFLER
SUGAR-GLAZED POTATOES

Excellent served with pork roast, chicken, duckling, ham, or other meat dishes. A classic Danish dish. Serves 4 to 6.

1 to 1½ lbs. cooked tiny new potatoes
4 Tbsp. sugar
¼ cup butter or margarine

Heat sugar in skillet until golden brown and without lumps. Add butter. Stir together.

Add the potatoes that have been rinsed in cold water (if using canned, drain, then add to skillet). The moisture helps caramelize the potatoes. The skillet must be fairly hot, so be careful not to burn the sugar mixture, it can get quite tricky. Turn the potatoes often while shaking the pan so they brown nicely on all sides. It will take approximately 10 minutes.

FINLAND

FINLAND

Finland, which is located in the northernmost section of Europe, is bordered by Sweden, Norway, and Russia. A third of Finland is within the Arctic Circle, and its northern part is in Lapland. As a neighbor to Sweden, Finland is influenced by both its language and culture. Swedish and Finnish are the official languages.

The climate in Finland reflects its northern latitude and affects the life style and diet of the Finnish people. Winters are extremely cold, with long nights from mid-November to the first of February. The summer growing season, though mostly daylight, is very short.

Finns are the products of nature. The location and climate of their country have forced them to be resourceful in raising, preserving, and preparing appropriate foods. They maintain deep storage bins or cellars to store potatoes and vegetables grown during the summers, and dried vegetables and fruits are amply used in soups, chowders, main dishes and desserts. They prepare foods for energy as well as for nourishment, adding lots of milk, cream, and buttermilk.

Fish, found abundantly in the seas and rivers of Finland, is an essential part of the Finnish diet. The Baltic herring is a favorite food. It is caught in large quantities during spring and summer when it is served fresh. Trout, salmon, and another favorite white fish, siika, are plentiful in the rivers of northern Finland. Crayfish are popular during the brief summer.

Many varieties of berries are found in Finland. Bright orange cloudberries grow in swampy areas, and blueberries and strawberries grow wild. A type of lingonberry, similar to our cranberry, is preserved in jams and preserves.

Each part of Finland has a favorite version of a sweet dough yeast bread called Pulla, served as a between-meal snack with coffee. It is a common custom to treat every drop-in visitor with coffee and Pulla. Finns are famous for their pastries. A special treat is the popular Christmas tart, Joulutorttu, its filling is made from dried prunes. Thin hot oven pancakes, Lätyt, form an important parts of the Finnish diet and are eaten either as a main course or dessert.

Many other unique specialties come from Finland, and others have
been adopted from their neighboring sister countries, all of which have
given her that genuine Scandinavian fame.

MAUSTESILLI - PICKLED HERRING

*This Scandinavian classic is best when refrigerated at least 24 hours.
Wonderful as an appetizer or fish course.*

3 salted herrings
2 red or yellow onions
1 cup white vinegar
¼ cup water
1 to 1½ cups sugar
½ tsp. white pepper
1 to 1½ Tbsp. pickling spice

Skin, bone and rinse the herring. Soak in cold water overnight. Drain
and cut into 1" pieces. Place in glass container. Make brine by
bringing to boil vinegar, sugar and spices. Cool. Pour brine over
herring fillets. Peel and slice onions thinly. Place over herring fillets
about 2 hours before serving.

Jos ei sauna ja viina ja terva
auta niin se tauti on kuolemaksi.

If a sauna, whisky and tar do not help,
the disease is fatal.

SIMA - LEMON POP

This is a refreshing drink in summer. Finns use it in place of soda pop.

9 qts. water
1 lb. white sugar
1 lb. brown sugar
2 lemons
1 Tbsp. yeast
raisins

Wash lemons. Peel yellow rind off thinly. Then remove white part and discard. Slice lemons very thinly. Boil water and pour over lemon and yellow peeling. Add sugar, stir, and let cool to lukewarm. Dissolve yeast in a little warm water and add to the cooled lemon water. Cover and let stand overnight. Strain into bottles. Put a little sugar and a few raisins into each bottle, then close with a cork. Place in a cool area and let stand for a few days. When soda is bubbly and not too sweet it is ready to enjoy. Store in refrigerator.

Note: Due to temperature and fermentation the bottles can become uncorked in the refrigerator. Check corks periodically.

KALJA - NON-ALCOHOLIC BEER

Kalja, a malt beverage/non-alcoholic beer, is a very popular drink in Finland. It is served with meals and after a sauna. Use a large clean plastic pail to prepare Kalja.

1 cup rye malt or malted barley grain
1 cup sugar
5 quarts boiling water
1 tsp. dry yeast

Mix the malt and sugar in the bottom of a pail and pour in the boiling water. When water has cooled to about 110° F, add the yeast. Cover with plastic wrap and allow to ferment at room temperature overnight. The next day, strain and bottle. Keep chilled until ready to serve.

KARJALAN PIIRAKAT - KARELIAN PASTIES

These pastries have long been traditional in a part of Eastern Finland called Karjala. After WWII their popularity spread throughout Finland. They are popular as a snack with coffee or tea as well as the buffet table. Traditionally topped with an Egg Butter. Makes 16.

Filling:

¾ cup medium grain rice
½ tsp. salt
1½ cups water
¾ cup milk
4 Tbsp. butter or margarine
1 egg, slightly beaten
¼ tsp. pepper

Dough:

1½ cups rye flour
1½ cups all-purpose flour
1 tsp. salt
2 Tbsp. melted butter or margarine
1 cup water

Butter Glaze:

¼ lb. butter
½ cup water or milk

Egg Butter:

4 hard-cooked eggs
¼ lb. butter
¼ tsp. salt
¼ tsp. pepper

Preheat oven to 475° F. Cook rice in salted water until water has been absorbed. Add milk and simmer until milk is absorbed. Add butter, egg, pepper, and stir. Adjust
seasoning.
While rice is cooking, mix all dry ingredients for dough in a bowl and mix in water gradually to make a firm bread dough. Flour surface well. Roll dough with hands into a 15-inch bar. Cut bar into 16 pieces. Roll out pieces into very thin circles. Sprinkle flour between circles. Brush off excess flour before filling with rice porridge.

Place 2 tablespoons of rice porridge lengthwise on center of crust, leaving sides empty. Fold and crimp edges with finger tips. The final shape is oval.

Prepare glaze, heat butter and water until butter is melted. Brush glaze lightly over pastries. Place on ungreased cookie sheet and bake for 15 minutes. Remove pasties from oven and brush again with glaze. Serve hot or cooled with egg butter.

While hard-cooked eggs are still warm, mash roughly together with softened butter. Blend in salt and pepper. Texture should be like scrambled eggs. Refrigerate only long enough to chill. Make egg butter shortly before serving. Serve pasties with egg butter on the side.

El kukaan ole mestari syntyisäs.

No one is a master at birth.

NÄKKILEIVÄT - SMALL RYE CRISP BREADS

A quick yeast bread. Makes 10 to 12 small breads.

1 Tbsp. yeast
1 cup water
1 tsp. salt
11/3 cups rye flour
11/3 cups all-purpose flour
ryemeal for rolling

Dissolve yeast in lukewarm water. Add salt and flours. Place a good heap of ryemeal on the board and shape dough into a roll, mixing in ryemeal as needed. Divide into 10 or 12 parts. Make into balls. Cover and let rise about 20 minutes. Roll each ball to about the size of a pancake. Then use textured rolling pin or prick each round with a fork. Place on cookie sheets and bake at 425° F for about 8 to 10 minutes, or until edges brown slightly.

Ei molemmille puolin voita leivälle.

Bread is not buttered on both sides.

PULLA "KRANSSI"
TRADITIONAL FINNISH COFFEE BREAD

Served for breakfast, brunch, dessert or snack. Makes one large ring or four to five braided breads.

Bread:
2½ (1/4 oz.) envelopes yeast
½ cup warm water
3 eggs
1 cup sugar
1½ tsp. salt
2 Tbsp. cardamom, crushed
2/3 cup melted butter or margarine
2 cups milk, scalded and cooled
9 to 10 cups unbleached flour
1 cup raisins

Topping:
1 egg
coarse sugar or almonds

Mix yeast in ½ cup warm water and let stand 5 minutes. In a large mixing bowl, beat eggs and sugar until light. Add yeast, salt, cardamom, melted butter and milk. Mix in 4 cups of flour and beat about 5 minutes. Add more flour, blending until it is too thick to mix. Sprinkle flour on a board, turn dough on it. Knead, adding flour as needed until dough is smooth and satiny. Place dough into a large greased bowl, cover with damp towel and let rise until double in bulk, about 1 hour.

Add raisins to dough if desired, and shape into 4 or 5 braided lengths or one large braid shaped into a round ring on a large cookie sheet. Cover and let rise until doubled.

Brush top with beaten egg or egg yolk diluted with water. Sprinkle with sugar or almonds. Bake at 375° F for 15 to 20 minutes, decrease temperature to 325° F and finish baking until golden brown, about 10 minutes.

PANNUKAKKU - OVEN BAKED PANCAKES

Serve these pancakes for breakfast with jam, crushed berries, syrup or honey and bacon. Delicious and quick to prepare for a busy morning. Or serve for a lunch or light supper. Serves 6 to 8.

4 eggs
1/3 cup granulated sugar
1½ cups flour
4 cups milk
1 tsp. salt

Preheat oven to 400° F. Use a 13"x9"x2" pan for thick pancakes and a large shallow pan for crustier pancakes. Beat eggs, add sugar, salt and flour. Mix until smooth. Add milk a little at a time and stir well until all milk is added and the batter is smooth. Pour into well-greased baking pan. Bake until brown, 15 to 25 minutes. Baking time depends upon the thickness of the batter. Cut the pancakes into serving pieces and serve hot.

TIIKERIKAKKU - TIGERCAKE

*An unusual marbled cake that uses a 1½ quart fluted cake pan.
Delicious!*

2/3 cup butter or margarine
1½ cups sugar
2 tsp. vanilla
3 eggs
2¼ cups all-purpose flour
2 tsp. baking powder
2/3 cup cream or milk
2 Tbsp. cocoa

Preheat oven to 350° F. Beat butter, sugar and vanilla until foamy.
Add eggs one at a time and beat well. Combine flour with baking
powder. Add cream, alternately with flour mixture. Stir well.

Pour half of the batter into another bowl. Mix in the cocoa. Put half of
the remaining light batter into a greased pan. Pour the cocoa batter
over and top with the other light batter, so that the dark batter is in the
middle. Cut the dough with a fork so that the cake will look marbled.
Bake for 1 hour.

Nauru pidentää ikää.

Laughter prolongs life.

LAPINKOTA - LAPPHUT

Named after the tepee-shaped home of the Lapps in northern Scandinavia.
A cake that is the edible part of a landscape. Serves 6 to 8.

Cake:

3 eggs
¾ cup sugar
1 tsp. baking powder
2/3 cup all-purpose flour

Preheat oven to 425° F. Beat the eggs and sugar together until light
and fluffy. Sift flour and baking powder together and fold lightly into
the egg/sugar mixture. Blend well. Spread onto a well-greased jelly
roll pan or lipped cookie sheet (10" x15"). Bake in oven for 7 minutes
or until done. Turn out onto waxed paper sprinkled generously with
granulated sugar. Immediately cut out three triangles, (about 7" wide
and 7" tall), from cake, using a sharp knife. Reserve rest of cake.

Glaze:

4 Tbsp. cocoa
4 Tbsp. powdered sugar
4 Tbsp. water

Boil all together until thick, then spread the glaze onto the three pieces
of triangular cake. Next make the filling.

Filling:

1 pint heavy cream, whipped and sweetened
1 (8 oz.) can fruit salad, drained or
1 small green apple, cored and chopped and
1 small red apple cored and chopped

To assemble:

Cut the reserved cake into bitesize pieces. Fold the cake and fruit into half of the whipped cream. Pile into the center of a serving dish, using a spatula, mounding the mixture up to about 7 inches high. This is the inside of the "hut". Place the chocolate glazed triangles against the mound with the chocolate side out, (this represents the soot-blackened sides of the hut!) Cover the seams with whipped cream. Make "snowdrifts" around the hut.

Dip a 5" to 6" birch twig (birch is preferred but not necessary) into the whipped cream and place it on top of the "hut" as the "smoke hole". Other twigs and small evergreens may be dipped into whipped cream and placed around to make a landscape.
To serve, slice from top to bottom of one side of the tepee shaped hut, remove cake and filling with a spatula.

EILA'S MUSTIKKAPIIRAKKA
EILA'S BLUEBERRY TORTE

*Fresh or frozen blueberries may be used for this wonderful warm dessert
torte. Serve this warm with whipped or ice cream on top. Makes 12
servings.*

2 eggs
1½ cups sugar
½ cup melted butter or margarine
1 cup half and half
2 tsp. baking powder
2½ cups flour, or as needed
6 cups blueberries
½ cup sugar

Preheat oven to 325° F. Beat the eggs with 1½ cups sugar until fluffy.
Add rest of liquid ingredients. Add baking powder. Add in flour until
a soft pourable batter is reached.

Pour into a well greased 9"x13" pan, spreading evenly. Cover with
blueberries. Sprinkle with ½ cup sugar. Bake about 30 minutes. Cut
into squares.

Note: If you use unthawed frozen blueberries, allow more cooking
time.

Mettä antaa, mitä mettäl on.

The forest gives what the forest has.

JOULUTORTUT - CHRISTMAS TARTS

Traditional special occasion and Christmas tarts. A variety of fruits may be used as filling.

5½ cups flour
1 lb. butter or margarine
1 tsp. salt
2 Tbsp. sugar
4 egg yolks
1 whole egg
1 cup cream or canned milk

Preheat oven to 375° F. In a large bowl sift flour, add butter, salt and sugar. Mix as for pie crust. Add egg yolks and whole egg, mixing well. Warm cream slightly and mix well into dough. Place in refrigerator for several hours.

Roll dough out to 1/8" thick. Cut into 3½" squares. Slash corners diagonally (about 1¼").

Filling:

2 lbs. pitted prunes, whole or chopped
¾ cup sugar
water
1 cinnamon stick

Cook prunes with sugar, cinnamon stick and water to cover. Cook until tender. Cool and remove cinnamon stick before using. Place 1 teaspoon filling in center of dough. Place every other corner over filling. Press firmly to make a pinwheel. Bake in preheated oven for 15 minutes.

Variation: DATE TARTS - substitute 1 lb. pitted dates for prunes. Increase sugar and water to 1 cup each and omit cinnamon stick. Proceed as directed.

RUNEBERGIN TORTUT - RUNEBERG'S TARTS

An interesting muffin variation of these classic Finnish tarts. Makes 24 muffins.

1 cup butter
1 cup sugar
2 eggs
1 cup chopped nuts
1 cup bread crumbs
½ cup flour
1 tsp. baking powder
jam, raspberry, preferably

Mix butter with sugar. Add eggs, 1 at a time. Mix nuts, bread crumbs, flour, and baking powder together and then add all at once to butter mixture.

Fill greased muffin pans two-thirds full. Make an indentation in top of each and fill with jam, smooth dough back.

Bake at 350° F for 10 to 15 minutes. When cold, remove from pans. Put ½ teaspoon jam on top of each muffin. Mix ½ cup powdered sugar and 1 teaspoon water for frosting and pipe it to form a ring around the jam.

HANNATÄDIN KAKUT - AUNT HANNA'S COOKIES

These "melt-in-your-mouth" cookies are fun to make when you have little visitors. Makes 4 to 5 dozen cookies.

1¾ cups butter or margarine
1¾ cups sugar
2/3 cup cream
2 to 2¼ cups flour
2/3 cup potato starch
2 tsp. baking powder

Preheat oven to 400° F. Cream butter with sugar until light. Add cream and mix in the sifted dry ingredients. Form small balls from the dough and place on cookie sheet. Bake until golden yellow, about 10 minutes.

RAPEAT PIPARKAKUT - CRISP GINGER COOKIES

This is an easy gingerbread cookie recipe to make. The dough is easy to handle, and the cookies are very crisp and delicious. Remember that gingerbread cookies improve with age. Resist the temptation to eat them right away! Makes 10 to 12 dozen cookies or if you double or triple the recipe, you will have enough dough to make a gingerbread house for Christmas!

½ lb. butter or margarine
½ cup dark (Karo) syrup
1 cup sugar
1 Tbsp. ground cloves
1 Tbsp. cinnamon
½ Tbsp. baking soda
2 Tbsp. water
1 lb. flour, or as needed

Preheat oven to 375° F. Heat the butter, syrup and sugar until butter is melted. Do not boil. Cool.

Mix in the other ingredients. Use enough flour for easy rolling of dough. Let dough rest, covered, preferably overnight. Roll out thinly and cut into cookie shapes. Bake 8 to 10 minutes or until done.

KUMINA PIPARKAKUT
CARAWAY SEED COOKIES

These are crispy and delicious cookies. Makes 5 to 6 dozen.

1 cup shortening
2 cups sugar
3 eggs
½ cup milk
1 tsp. lemon extract
½ tsp. almond extract
4 cups flour
¼ tsp. salt
1 tsp. caraway seed, crushed
1 tsp. nutmeg

Preheat oven to 375° F. Cream shortening and sugar. Add eggs and beat for one minute. Add rest of ingredients. Mix well. Chill the dough. Roll out very thin on a floured board. Cut into small circles. Set one inch apart on a greased baking sheet and bake in oven for 10 minutes.

KARPALOPUURO - CRANBERRY WHIP

Early childhood memories come to mind when this traditional and pretty pink dessert is served. Makes 4 servings.

2 cups cranberries
3 cups water
1 cup sugar
6 Tbsp. Cream of Wheat

Boil cranberries and water until skin breaks. Put through strainer. Add water to make 3 cups juice. Add sugar. Bring back to boil, then add Cream of Wheat slowly, stirring constantly. Cook 20 minutes, stirring constantly. Remove from heat. Pour into bowl. Whip until mixture is pale pink. Serve with cream.

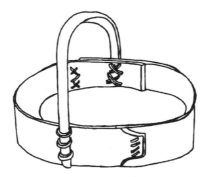

LUUMUKIISSELI - PRUNE DESSERT

A traditional Sunday dessert! Serve chilled with whipped cream. Makes 4 to 6 servings.

1 lb. dried prunes or mixed dried fruit
5 cups water
½ cup sugar
1 stick cinnamon
1 Tbsp. potato starch
2 Tbsp. water
½ lemon
1 cup raisins, optional

Rinse the prunes in warm water. Cover with water and let soak for a few hours or overnight. Add sugar, lemon and cinnamon. Add more water if necessary. Cover and cook until the prunes are soft.

Remove the prunes to a bowl. Thicken the liquid with a mixture of potato starch and 2 tablespoons cold water and let boil briefly. Pour over the prunes and sprinkle water on top.

LINDSTRÖMIN PIHVIT - BEEF A'LA LINDSTRÖM

Serve with juices from the frying pan, potatoes, green salad, ketchup or mustard. The unusual flavorings make this fit for a king! Makes 4 servings.

1 lb. ground beef
2 boiled and mashed potatoes
1 egg, beaten
salt, to taste
white pepper, to taste
1/3 to 2/3 cup finely chopped, pickled beets
2 Tbsp. finely chopped onion
2 Tbsp. capers
1 Tbsp. butter or margarine
1/3 cup water

Mix meat, potato, egg and spices. Add liquid, mix. Add beets, onion, and capers. Mix well and make into four 1" thick patties. Brown butter in a frying pan. Fry the patties quickly on both sides until done. Remove patties and deglaze the pan with a small amount of water. Check and adjust the seasonings.

MAKSAPIHVIT - FRIED LIVER

A tasty way to prepare liver with onions in a cream sauce.   *Makes 4 servings.*

1 to 1½ lbs. sliced beef or calf liver
2 to 3 yellow onions, sliced
2 to 3 Tbsp. butter or margarine
salt, to taste
white pepper, to taste
1 Tbsp. flour
½ to 1 cup cream

Sauté onion in part of the butter until soft. Remove from skillet. Melt remainder of butter until just golden, add the liver, and brown on both sides. Season. Remove from skillet.

Cream Sauce:
Sprinkle flour on top of remaining drippings in skillet. Stir. Add cream. Cook covered over low heat a few minutes. Add liver. Serve with onions on top. Sprinkle with parsley.

KAALIKÄÄRYLEET - CABBAGE ROLLS

A traditional Finnish cabbage dish. Serve with lingonberry or cranberry sauce. Makes 8 servings.

1 large head of cabbage
salt, to taste
water
¾ cup rice
1 cup water

Meat Filling:

1 lb. ground beef
¼ cup melted butter or margarine
¼ cup bread crumbs
½ cup water
¾ cup cream
salt, to taste
white pepper, to taste
1 Tbsp. brown sugar or syrup
½ Tbsp. salt
bouillon or water
½ cup cream

Cut the core from the head of cabbage. Boil the cabbage in salted water until leaves are pliable and transparent, about 10 minutes. Remove from water and drain. Remove the leaves and cut off excess thickness of leaves.

Boil rice in salted water until done, about 15 minutes. Cool. Add melted butter or margarine, bread crumbs, water, cream, and spices to the meat. Mix well. Add the meat mixture to the cooled rice. Mix well. The smallest cabbage leaves are chopped up and added to the rice-meat mixture. Place 1 tablespoonful of this filling on each cabbage leaf, which are then wrapped, package fashion.

Continued next page

Place in a greased, shallow baking dish, side by side, seam side down. Sprinkle salt and brown sugar or syrup on top and bake for about 1 hour in 350° F oven. Turn occasionally and pour water over to keep them moist. Place cabbage rolls on a platter. Make a gravy of cream and bouillon or liquid from the cabbage.

KARJALANPAISTI - KARELIAN POT ROAST

One of the most traditional Finnish dishes. Quick and easy preparation makes this wonderful for a buffet dish. Serve directly from the pot, with boiled potatoes and a hearty rye bread. Makes 10 to 12 servings.

1 lb. beef
1 lb. lamb
1 lb. pork
   (add kidney or liver if desired)
2 tsp. salt
water
whole allspice, chopped onion, bay leaf, optional*

Use any cut of meat, but meat intended for roasting is best. Cut meat into serving pieces. Layer them with salt into an ovenproof pot. Add water to cover. Place in medium hot oven. Cook until tender, 2 to 3 hours, at 350° F oven.

Note: True Karelian pot roast is seasoned with salt only, but if desired, you may add allspice, onion and bay leaf.

SILAKKAKÄÄRYLEET - SMELT ROLLS

A very old Finnish recipe. Serve with potatoes and a sauce made with mayonnaise and horseradish. Makes 8 to 10 servings.

1¾ lbs. smelt
1 tsp. salt
dill weed, fresh if available

For boiling:

¾ cup water
¾ cup white distilled vinegar
1 tsp. salt
5 whole white peppercorn
5 whole allspice
1 to 2 bay leaves

Clean the fish and remove the spine. Rinse the fillets. Put on a cutting board with skin down. Sprinkle on salt and place a branch of fresh dill on each fillet. Roll the fillets tightly and place side by side in the bottom of a pot.

Combine the ingredients for boiling and boil briefly. Check for seasoning. Pour over the fish. Let the fish cook on low heat. Do not overcook. Let cool in the liquid.

Remove the fish rolls. Place in serving dish. Decorate with dill.

Kaunis on kala vedessä, kaunihimpi kattilassa.

**A fish is beautiful in the water,
but more beautiful in the pan.**

ROSOLLI - BEET & HERRING SALAD

A traditional vegetable salad that is made for all important family gatherings. Serve the colorful dressing on the side. Makes 6 servings.

1 lb. potatoes
1 lb. carrots
½ lb. beets (without tops)
½ cup diced onion
½ cup diced dill pickle
½ cup salt herring, chopped
¼ tsp. salt, optional
freshly ground white pepper, to taste
1 clove garlic, pressed

Peel potatoes, carrots and beets. Plunge potatoes and carrots in salted boiling water. Cook for about 20 minutes or until done. Drain and allow to cool before dicing. Submerge beets in salted boiling water. Cook for 30 minutes or until done. Drain, reserve 2 tablespoons beet water. Allow to cool before dicing.

Mix all ingredients. Add salt, pepper and pressed garlic; toss. Refrigerate.

Dressing:

¾ cup heavy cream
1 Tbsp. sugar
½ tsp. salt
2 Tbsp. vinegar
1 Tbsp. dry mustard
2 Tbsp. beet juice for coloring

Whip heavy cream until it thickens slightly. Add remaining dressing ingredients, mixing well.

VIHREÄ SALAATTI KERMA-KASTIKKEELLA
GREEN SALAD WITH CREAM DRESSING

Wonderful with the first greens from the garden. Makes 6 servings.

1 head butter or leaf lettuce
1 cucumber

Dressing:

2 eggs
1 Tbsp. sugar
½ tsp. salt
1 tsp. mustard
2 Tbsp. vinegar or lemon juice
¾ cup heavy cream, lightly beaten

Rinse and dry the salad leaves. Slice cucumber.

Boil the eggs and separate yolks and whites. Mash egg yolks. Add sugar, salt and mustard, vinegar or lemon juice, and cream. Pour dressing over the salad leaves and cucumber slices before serving, sprinkle with chopped egg whites.

MAITOKAALI - CABBAGE SOUP WITH MILK

A creamy, old-fashioned soup thats delicious on a cold winters night. Makes 6 to 8 servings.

2½ lbs. cabbage
2 cups water
2 Tbsp. butter or margarine
1 Tbsp. flour
2 qts. milk
6 whole allspice
1 bay leaf
sugar, to taste
salt, to taste

Chop the cabbage finely, add water and cook until almost tender.

In small saucepan, melt butter or margarine. Stir in flour, then hot milk a little at a time. Add sauce to cabbage. Add allspice and bay leaf and simmer until the cabbage is soft. Add sugar and salt to taste.

HEDELMÄKIISSELI - DRIED FRUIT SOUP

This thick "soup" is served cold with dollops of whipped cream. Some add a dash of lemon juice to this soup. Makes 6 to 8 servings.

7 oz. mixed dried fruit
8 cups water
1 cinnamon stick
½ cup sugar
2 Tbsp. potato starch
4 Tbsp. cold water

Wash the dried fruit and soak in cold water overnight. Boil fruits in the same water, adding cinnamon and sugar. Cook over low heat until the fruit is soft. Add potato starch that has been dissolved in cold water. Bring to a boil, stirring; remove from heat.

KALAKEITTO - FISH SOUP OR STEW

A traditional milk-based fish soup or stew. Makes 6 to 8 servings.

2 lbs. peeled potatoes, cut in chunks
2½ cups milk
salt and pepper to taste
1 medium onion, peeled
1 bay leaf
1 lb. boneless, skinless whiting,
  cut in large pieces
1 lb. boneless, skinless scrod,
  cut in large pieces
1 lb. boneless, skinless salmon or
  flounder, cut in large pieces
½ cup heavy cream
4 Tbsp. butter
1 generous handful fresh dill, chopped

Boil potatoes in milk until done. Add salt and pepper. Slice onion and place in another saucepan with bay leaf. Add fish, cover almost entirely with water. Bring to a boil and simmer until fish becomes flaky.

Transfer fish pieces to potatoes and milk. Add strained fish liquid. Adjust seasoning. Add cream, butter, and chopped dill while soup is still hot. Serve immediately.

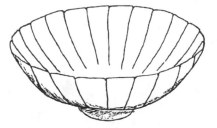

KESÄKEITTO - SUMMER SOUP

A wonderful summer soup when fresh garden vegetables are used. Try small new potatoes, carrots, peas and peapods. In winter a variety of frozen vegetables may be used.

2 carrots
1 leek
1 parsnip
1 stalk of celery

or:

1 small cauliflower or new potatoes
1 carrot
1 cup peas or 1 (10 oz.) pkg. of frozen peas
½ to ¾ qts. of water
dash salt or to taste
1 to 2 Tbsp. flour
1 pint milk
white pepper
parsley or dill

Wash vegetables, dice or slice. Add to boiling, salted water and let cook until almost done. Frozen peas need only 10 minutes cooking time. Leek should be added just 5 minutes before the other vegetables are done.

Mix flour with a small amount of milk and pour into the soup, stirring carefully. Let cook 3 to 5 minutes. Add the remainder of the milk and heat. Add parsley or dill.

Note: Soup may also be thickened with an egg yolk and cream instead of milk and flour.

HERNEKEITTO - PEA SOUP

*In some parts of the country this hearty yellow pea soup is the Thursday
evening meal. Quicker split peas may be used instead. Makes 6 servings.*

¾ lb. dried, yellow, whole peas*
2 qts. water
½ to 1 lb. slightly salted ham shoulder, flank or loin
1 onion, chopped
marjoram, thyme, or ginger, to taste
salt, to taste

Soak the peas in water about 12 hours. Let boil in the same water.
Remove foam and skins that rise to the top. Cube the meat and add to
the soup. Add onion and spices. Cook slowly until the peas are soft
and the meat is tender; about 1½ hours.

KAUHAVAN PIHVI KEITTO
BEEF STEW WITH ROOT VEGETABLES

*Some prefer the light-colored stew with plenty of liquid. Serve with
homemade bread or steam dumplings over the stew. Makes 4 servings.*

1 lb. beef stew meat, cut into small pieces
2 Tbsp. butter
4 cups water or more
4 whole allspice
1 small rutabaga, peeled and diced
3 medium potatoes, peeled and coarsely chopped
2 onions, peeled and sliced
3 carrots, peeled and diced
salt, to taste

In soup pot, brown beef lightly in butter. Add water and allspice,
simmer until beef is tender, about one hour. Add vegetables and salt,
continue to simmer about 30 minutes or until vegetables are done, not
mushy.

PORKKANALAATIKKO - CARROT CASSEROLE

A traditional casserole dish for holidays, weddings or other special family events. Goes well with turkey and ham. Makes about 6 servings.

½ cup rice
1 cup water
2 cups milk
1 lb. carrots
sugar, to taste
salt, to taste
1 egg, beaten
bread crumbs, to taste
butter

Cook the rice in the water for 15 minutes. Add the cold milk and let cool. Add peeled and shredded carrots, spices and egg. Pour into a greased, ovenproof dish. Sprinkle with bread crumbs and dot with bits of butter.
Bake until set, about 40 minutes in 390° F oven.

PINAATTIMUHENNOS - CREAMED SPINACH

Serve with egg, fish or meat dishes. Makes 4 servings.

1½ lbs. fresh spinach, or 1 pkg. frozen spinach
water
1½ Tbsp. butter or margarine
3 Tbsp. flour
1¼ cups milk, scalded
salt, white pepper, nutmeg

Rinse the fresh spinach. Boil in a little water for 5 minutes. Drain. Chop fine. Melt butter, stir in the flour and add hot milk, a little at a time. Cook 3 to 5 minutes. Add the spinach. Season.

LANTTULAATIKKO - RUTABAGA CASSEROLE

Rutabaga has an interesting flavor and this Finnish favorite makes the most of it. Serve with meats. It is usually on holiday menus. Makes 4 to 6 servings.

2 lbs. rutabagas
water to cover
salt, to taste
2 cups half and half
1/3 cup bread crumbs
1 onion
3 Tbsp. Golden or Light Karo syrup

salt and nutmeg, to taste
¼ cup butter
2 eggs

Peel, cut in cubes and boil the rutabagas in salted water until soft. Save the boiling water. Mash the rutabagas and add the boiling water, bread crumbs that have been soaked in half and half, onions, syrup, spices, butter, and eggs.

Put mixture into a greased ovenproof dish and sprinkle bread crumbs on top. Bake for about 1 hour in 350° F oven.

El rakkaus ruastu.

Love does not rust.

ICELAND

ICELAND

"An Island In The Middle Of An Ocean"

Iceland is located near the middle of the North Atlantic Ocean. This somewhat isolated island is larger than Ireland. It was the last European country to be settled and became an independent republic on June 17, 1944, when it was separated from the Danish crown.

Surprisingly, ice covers only about one-eighth of Iceland! The island boasts of a cool, temperate climate since its northerly latitude is counteracted by warm breezes from the Gulf Stream. Winds do become severe and cold at times, but are moderate during the summer when inland areas may even be quite warm.

Hot springs connected with extensive volcanic activity are found all over Iceland in the form of steam, boiling water, sulphur, etc. This natural heat is widely used in greenhouses, homes, buildings, and swimming pools. Hardly any trees or shrubs are found in Iceland, and only one native wild animal, the Arctic fox, although a few reindeer, originally brought from Norway, are found in eastern areas.

The sea surrounding Iceland has an abundance of various fish, particularly herring, cod, ocean perch, haddock, plaice, and halibut. Trout and salmon abound in the rivers and lakes. Eighty percent of Iceland's exports consist of fish and fish-related products.

The heavy-wooled Icelandic sheep are numerous. Hence, lamb and mutton are a chief meat product. Recently, cattle-raising and dairying have increased in importance. Poultry farms supply an abundance of eggs, yet chicken is not eaten a great deal. The only game is the Icelandic mountain ptarmigan, or rjúpa, resembling a quail, though its plumage is white in winter. The meat is dark with a strong gamey flavor.

Potatoes and root vegetables are grown in greenhouses year-round with tomatoes, cucumbers, and lettuce. Green vegetables are available fresh only in summer. They are dried or preserved for use in winter. Most fruits are imported. Breads, mostly rye, Hverabraud, are baked in natural hot springs.

The beer in Iceland is bjór and pilsner. They are very low in alcoholic content with a refreshing taste. Most popular of the strong drinks is the Icelandic brennivin or schnaps.

Fortitude and hardwork were, and still are, the tools of the Icelanders. Merriment and "good food" is still their reward. Over the decades "good food" has escalated the culinary atributes of the Icelander to a competitive stature within the European community. The recipes in this book represent a bit of the old and the new Icelandic cuisine.

FLATBRAUD - FLAT BREAD

An old receipe for a traditional bread. Spread with butter. Good with smoked lamb, paté, cheese, or smoked herring.

1 lb. rye flour
1 to 1¼ cups boiling water

Wet flour with boiling water and knead. Divide dough into parts big enough to make thin round cakes about the size of a dessert plate. Bake on a cast iron griddle (very hot) and turn frequently.

Note: Rye flour can be mixed with white flour, if preferred.

LUMMUR - RICE FRITTERS

Served hot with jelly, these are a treat.

1½ cups rice
1 cup water
1 tsp. salt
2 eggs, beaten
¼ cup all-purpose flour
2 qts. milk
2 tsp. cinnamon
¼ cup chopped almonds
¼ cup currants
1 tsp. grated lemon rind
butter for the frying pan

Put rice and water in a saucepan. After coming to a boil, drain off the liquid. Boil the milk in another saucepan. Add the rice and stir until it starts boiling. When the salt has been added, put the lid on the saucepan and simmer for 1 hour. Cool for 15 minutes.

Add the beaten eggs, then the flour to rice. Mix well. Finally, add the almonds, cinnamon, currants, and the lemon rind. Drop the batter by teaspoonfuls into the melted butter on a frying pan. Brown the fritters on both sides.

PÖNNUKOKUR - ICELANDIC CREPES

A sweet crepe that is usually filled with jam and whipped cream. Delicious! Makes 45 to 50 crepes.

6 eggs
½ cup sugar
1 cup milk
¼ tsp. salt
1 cup all-purpose flour
½ tsp. baking powder
1 Tbsp. butter, melted
1 tsp. cardomom

Beat eggs until light. Add rest of ingredients, beating well. Batter should be very thin. Bake on a crepe pan.

GRJONAGRAUTUR - RICE PORRIDGE

This is good served hot or cold.

2 pints milk
1 pint water
1 tsp. salt
½ cup rice
cinnamon-sugar mixture

Let the rice boil in the water for 15 minutes. Then boil slowly with milk for 30 minutes. Add salt. Sprinkle the servings with cinnamon-sugar mixture.

MYSUOSTUR - ICELANDIC WHEY CHEESE

This "special" cheese recipe from Iceland is spread on bread like jam.

2 gallons milk
1 tsp. liquid rennet
1 cup sugar
1 cup thick cream or 4 Tbsp. butter

Warm milk and add rennet. When set, break up curd and strain it off. Boil whey down until about 1 pint remains (takes nearly a whole day), then strain. Add cream or butter, or both may be added if desired. Cook for 30 minutes. Then beat thoroughly until cold. If it is not beaten thoroughly, it becomes coarse and sandy. It should be smooth and creamy and thick enough to spread on bread like jam.

**En orztirr deyr aldregi,
hveim er sér góðan getr.**

**One thing I know never dies,
the reputation of a good man.**

SKYR - DESSERT OF SOUR MILK

Skyr is the Icelandic version of yogurt but with a stronger flavor. It was brought to Iceland by the Norwegians when Iceland was settled. Now one can buy it ready made in all dairy shops there. Use Bjetti when Skyr is not available.

4 qts. sweet milk
2 Tbsp. bjetti or skyr
12 drops rennet

Take the sweet milk and bring it to a boil. Cool until lukewarm. Take ½ cup milk and stir in 2 tablespoons bjetti. Stir this into the lukewarm milk. Add the rennet, stir well. Set aside in a warm place about 24 hours. Drain off liquid through cheese cloth. Remove from cheese cloth, put in bowl, beat well and serve with cream, sweetened with sugar if desired.

BJETTI:

2 eggs, well beaten
½ cup sour cream
1 Tbsp. sugar

Beat all ingredients well.

JOLAKAKA - CHRISTMAS LOAF

An easy-to-make and exceptionally flavorful pound cake. Makes 1 loaf.

1 cup butter or margarine
1 cup sugar
4 eggs
1 ½ cups all-purpose flour
1 tsp. cardamom powder
½ cup raisins
½ cup chocolate chips
grated rind of one orange

Cream butter and sugar. Add one egg at a time while continuing with the creaming. Add cardamom and flour, beating until blended. Stir in raisins, chocolate and orange rind. Pour the batter into a greased large tin or loaf pan (9x5x3 inches). Bake for 50 to 60 minutes at 350° F. Test with toothpick in center of loaf for doneness.

ICELANDIC VINARTERTA - ICELANDIC TORT

*The VINARTERTA is very rich and incredibly delicious -- ideal
for the holiday season!*

1 cup butter
1½ cups fine grain sugar
2 large eggs
4 cups all-purpose flour
1 tsp. baking powder
1 tsp. ground cardamom
½ tsp. almond extract
2 tsp. cream

Preheat oven to 375° F. Cream the butter, adding sugar gradually and
eggs one at a time. Sift the dry ingredients together and work into the
first mixture, adding flavoring and cream. Knead in all the flour and
divide dough into five equal parts. Pat each part into a 9" round cake
pan and bake until golden brown (about 10 minutes). Remove from pan
while still hot as they become quite hard. Cool.

Filling:

1 lb. prunes
1 cup sugar
1 Tbsp. cinnamon
½ cup water
1 tsp. vanilla or brandy

Boil the prunes, drain (save the liquid). Put prunes through grinder to
make a paste. Combine the paste with the sugar, cinnamon and flavoring,
adding a half cup of the prune liquid. Reduce the mixture, stirring
constantly, until a spreadable consistancy. Cool.

To construct the tort, alternate layers of cake and filling. Then wrap it
in a brandy- or red wine-soaked cloth and let stand for five days in a cool
place. May be topped with whipped cream if desired.

KOKOSDROPAR
COCONUT CREAM CHEESE COOKIES

Use your favorite kind of nuts. Makes 3 to 4 dozen.

1 cup butter
1¼ cup cream cheese
1¼ cup granulated sugar
1 egg
2 Tbsp. milk
¼ tsp. vanilla
1½ cup flour
1 cup coconut flakes
¼ cup chopped nuts

In a large mixing bowl cream together butter, cream cheese and sugar. Mix in egg, milk and vanilla. Beat until fluffy. Blend in flour and coconut. Stir mixture until well combined.

Drop rounded teaspoons of dough on a greased cookie sheet 2 inches apart. Sprinkle cookie dough with nuts. Bake at 350°F for 18 to 20 minutes. Cool slightly before removing from pan.

LAUFABRAUD - LEAFTHIN COOKIES

These cookies are traditionally served at Christmastime.

1 lb. all-purpose flour
1 tsp. baking powder
1 Tbsp. butter
1 Tbsp. sugar
1 cup hot milk

Mix flour, baking powder and butter so well that it can be sifted. Sift mixture into a large bowl and add sugar and hot milk. Knead dough. Cut in half and roll each part out until very thin. Cut out rounds as big as dessert plates. Let cool about ½ hour. With a sharp knife, cut decoration designs into the cookies. Deep fry until golden on both sides. Drain on paper toweling.

RABARBARASUPA - RHUBARB SOUP

Rhubarb is cultivated in many a backyard in Iceland and used for making jam and syrup, sweet soup, and pudding. Serve as a dessert accompanied with hard biscuits.

5 cups water
1 lb. fresh rhubarb
sugar to taste
1 Tbsp. potato flour or cornstarch

Wash rhubarb stalks and cut into small pieces. Boil rhubarb in the water for 5 minutes. Sweeten. Take off heat and stir in potato flour already dissolved in water.

RABARBARAGRAUTUR MED RYÖMA
RHUBARB PUDDING WITH CREAM

Easy to make, simply good. Serve with table cream or milk.

1 lb. rhubarb
2½ cups water
2 to 3 Tbsp. potato flour
sugar to taste

Wash rhubarb stalks and cut into small pieces. Boil rhubarb in the water for 5 minutes. Sweeten. Take off heat and stir in potato flour already dissolved in water.

RULLUPYLSÆ - BAKED MEATROLL

Baked flavor and ease make this lamb recipe stand out. Very good served on Flatbread.

2¼ lbs. thin breasts of lamb
1 Tbsp. salt
1 tsp. pepper
2 Tbsp. chopped onion

Trim the meat, remove gristle and small bones. Sprinkle the spices and onion over the whole surface of the meat and roll it up. Tie up the roll securely using cotton string. Put the roll in a 350° F oven for 1½ hours in an oven bag.

Allow the roll to cool before the meat is cut into thin slices.

RULLUPYLSÆ - ROLLED SAUSAGE

This has a unique and wonderful flavor. Makes excellent open-faced sandwiches on brown bread or flatbread.

1 to 2 small onions
2 Tbsp. salt
¼ tsp. saltpeter
½ tsp. cloves
1 tsp. allspice
½ tsp. pepper
4½ lbs. mutton or lamb flank with bones removed.

Chop 1 or 2 small onions finely, mix with spices. Fix mutton so that lean and fat alternate. Sprinkle with onion and spices.

Roll and hold with fork while sewing. Tie tightly with string and keep rolled in clean cloth for a day or two in the refrigerator to season. If lamb, boil 2 hours, and if mutton, boil 2½ hours. Place under weight until firmly pressed.

KÆEFA - ICELANDIC HEADCHEESE

A homemade Scandinavian favorite lunchmeat. Tastes so good!

3 lbs. veal
3 lbs. lamb
enough water to cover meat
2 large onions
1 tsp. pepper
1 tsp. ginger
2 tsp. allspice
2 Tbsp. salt

Boil meat for three hours, then remove bones and put meat through meat grinder. Take meat juice and add onions that have been put through a grinder. Add all spices. Put meat back into meat juice and boil for 15 to 20 minutes. Pour into form to cool, then slice and serve.

SODID HANGIKJÖT - BOILED SMOKED LAMB

Traditionally served on Christmas Day with creamed potatoes, peas, and Laufabraud. Serve Smoked Lamb cold.

2 lbs. smoked lamb
3 pints water

Brush the meat with tepid water. Put the meat into boiling water. Let meat boil for 45 minutes and then cool in the saucepan.

En morgum teksk verr en vill, ok verôr pat morgum,
. . at pa fá eigi alls gætt jafnvel, er honum er mikit í skapi.

But many a man docs worse than he intends,
and it happens with many a one that he can't think
of everything when he has much on his mind.

STEIKTAR RJUPUR - SAUTEED PTARMIGAN

Quail or Cornish Game Hens may be substituted for Ptarmigan. Serve accompanied with sugar-browned potatoes, red cabbage, small green peas and apple salad. Good served with the rich gravy recipe below.

Ptarmigan, quail or Cornish Game Hens
butter
bacon
salt and pepper, to taste
juniper berries

In a large skillet, fry the skinned and cleaned ptarmigan in butter with some bacon until golden brown. Season with salt, pepper, and juniper berries.

Place the ptarmigan in a Dutch oven or large saucepan, pour drippings from frying pan over and add a little boiling water. Let simmer for about 1 hour. Remove the ptarmigan from Dutch oven when tender and take out the breast bones.

Keep the ptarmigan warm in oven while making the gravy. Wrap in aluminum foil so meat does not dry out. Put the bones back into the Dutch oven with the broth and boil a little longer.

RICH GRAVY: Strain the broth, bring back to a boil, and thicken with flour mixed with a little water. Add salt, pepper and red currant jelly to taste. Just before serving, add a bit of whipped cream for extra richness.

STEIKT SILD - FRIED HERRING

Sprinkle the herring with vinegar and serve hot with boiled potatoes.

3 lbs. herring
1 Tbsp. salt
3 Tbsp. flour
1 Tbsp. vinegar
butter, margarine or oil for the frying pan

Roll the cleaned herring in salted flour and fry it. Small herrings may keep the heads on. Pan fry.

át ek i hvild
áôr ek heiman fór
sildr ok hafra;
saôr em ek enn pess.

I ate in peace
before I left home
herring and oatmeal;
so that I am still well-fed.

SALTFISKUR - SALT COD

An ancient and simple recipe that is good served with Onion Buttersauce and boiled potatoes.

Dry salted cod
enough water to cover

Soak dry salted cod in cold water for 24 hours. Then boil the fish for about 20 minutes, drain off salty water.

ONION BUTTERSAUCE: Mix fresh or sauteed chopped onion with melted butter.

NORWAY

NORWAY

Smörgåsbord in Norway is called a "koldt bord". This elaborate buffet consists of a magnificent variety of fish, cold meats, cheeses, salads, and desserts.

Norway has a long coastline, making seafood an important food in the Norwegian diet. Cod, herring, and shell fish are abundant. Norwegian tables feature boiled codfish and lutefish (prepared from dried codfish which has been soaked in lye). The latter is said to contain no calories, and girls are told they will be pretty from eating it. Fish is also used as an ingredient in puddings, souffles, and mousses. It is ground sometimes as many as seven times to produce a velvety smooth texture. Canned Norwegian fish balls are a popular import to the United States.

Potatoes have been a blessing to the Norwegians since the 1800s. At that time the people struggled through long, cold winters. Church pastors urged their parishioners to plant potatoes to avoid starvation. From the potato came potato flour, potato starch, and potato cakes (Potato Lefse). Boiled potatoes mixed with flour, called Raspeballer, or kumle, are served with saltmeat and vegetables. Leftover potato balls are enjoyed fried and eaten with a jam called Tyttebærsyltetøy, or with syrup and melted butter.

Common among meats are pork, reindeer, and mutton, as well as smoked and dried meats. Norway's national meat dish is lamb and cabbage, Får i Kål. A popular Norwegian cheese is a hard, brown goat cheese called Geitost.

Unique in Norway is Krumkake, a Christmas cookie, baked in a special iron griddle and rolled in a cone while still hot and soft. Rømmegrøt is a porridge of sour cream used on festive occasions. Rice pudding is served in Norway, Denmark, and Sweden on Christmas Eve. In one portion, an almond is customarily hidden. In Norway and Denmark, the lucky finder is given a little marzipan pig or similar prize, while in Sweden the finder is assumed to be the next one to get married. A delicious, deep-fried cookie, called Fattigmann in Norway and Sweden, is widely prepared at Christmas time.

JULEBRØD - CHRISTMAS BREAD

*Rich, traditional Scandinavian Christmas bread is fragrant with
cardamom and studded with citron and raisins. Treat your family and
friends to this homemade treasure.*

1 cup butter
¾ cup sugar
2 eggs
2 egg yolks
2 crushed cardamom seeds or 2 tsp. ground cardamom
1 cup milk
2 oz. yeast or 2 Tbsp. dry yeast
3½ to 4 cups all-purpose flour
2/3 cup citron
2/3 cup raisins

Cream butter and sugar. Whip eggs and egg yolks together. Add eggs
and cardamom to creamed mixture. Dissolve yeast in lukewarm milk.
(If using dry yeast, dissolve in ¼ cup warm water with a pinch of
sugar.) Add the yeast mixture gradually to creamed mixture
alternating with the sifted flour. The dough should be worked well.
Let rise for 3 hours. Punch dough down and knead together with the
finely cut citron and raisins. Put into a well-greased cake pan and let
rise until double in bulk. Brush with egg white. Bake in preheated
oven at 350° F for 1 hour.

Øvelse gjør mester.

Practice makes one a master.

FASTELAVENSBOLLER - BUNS FOR LENT

Traditionally served for breakfast with coffee on Fastelavens (Sunday). Table decorations should be a bouquet of leafless twigs with multi-colored ribbons attached. Makes 24 buns.

1 oz. cake yeast or ¼ oz. pkg. dry yeast
1 cup milk
1/3 cup butter or margarine
2 Tbsp. sugar
2 cups all-purpose flour
2 tsp. cardamom
1 egg white

Add the yeast to the lukewarm milk, stir until dissolved. Add butter, sugar, and knead in the flour. Save a little for rolling out. Let rise in warm place for about 30 minutes. On a floured kitchen table, roll out the dough, not too thin. Cut into approximately 10 squares. In the middle of each square, put one
tablespoon of filling.

Filling:

2 Tbsp. sugar, mixed with
2 Tbsp. butter
2 to 3 Tbsp. raisins, chopped
20 almonds, chopped

Fold the corners into the middle of the dough, over the filling. Place the buns on a greased cookie sheet, with the folds toward the cookie sheet. Brush with slightly beaten egg white, let rise for about 20 minutes. Brush again with egg white. Bake in preheated oven, 425° to 450° F, for about 10 to 12 minutes.

After the buns have cooled, cut them in half, put a little whipped cream between the two halves. Decorate with whipped cream and strips of candied orange peel, or sprinkle the buns with sifted powdered sugar.

HARDANGERLEFSE - LEFSE I

Lefse originated in Hardanger, western Norway. It is now served throughout Norway on any social occasion. If you don't have the modern electric lefse grill, they may be baked on a pancake griddle. Serve with butter, sugar and cinnamon. Makes about 16 sheets.

2 cups buttermilk
½ cup sugar
½ cup white corn syrup
all-purpose flour
2 tsp. soda, added to the buttermilk
3 beaten eggs
2 tsp. salt

Combine ingredients, adding enough flour to make a stiff dough. Roll out on floured board, using a rolling pin. Bake on lefse-grill. Soften lefse by wrapping in a damp cloth before using. Fold over, and cut into serving pieces.

De dummeste bøndene får de største potetene.

The most stupid peasants get the biggest potatoes.

LEFSE II

This is a soft bread. It may be served with creamed butter and powdered sugar or simply with butter alone or with sugar and cinnamon added. Sometimes it is served with Geitost. Makes 30 sheets.

½ cup lard or shortening
1 Tbsp. salt
4 cups all-purpose flour
4 cups milk, scalded

Add lard, salt and 2 cups of flour to scalded milk and mix well over low heat. Remove from fire. Sift 2 cups of flour onto board, add warm dough and work in flour. Knead well and cool.

Dough can be rolled immediately or kept in a cool place for a couple of days. Make a small patty. Flour board lightly and with a rolling pin, roll patty in all directions, keeping the dough round. Roll lightly, stretching dough until it is almost as big as the lefse-grill or baker. Transfer to the baker (pancake griddle), prick air bubbles and brown lightly. Turn and brown the other side. Cut each sheet into 4 pieces.

POTETESKAKER - POTATO LEFSE

In some Eastern sections of Norway this is called "Lumper". During World War II Potato Lefse supplemented the Norwegians skimpy rations. Serve with butter and syrup, or butter only, as preferred. May be served hot or cold. Makes 10 cakes.

6 potatoes, peeled and quartered
all-purpose flour
2 tsp. salt

Boil potatoes until done, drain, then mash finely and let cool. Add salt and flour, enough to make a stiff dough. Mix well. Form into cakes the size of a large pancake, about ¼" thick. Cook on top of stove or on a pancake griddle until well done. Turn cakes so they will bake evenly on both sides.

NORSKE VAFLER - MORS VAFLER
MOTHER'S SOUR CREAM WAFFLES

These Norwegian waffles are often enjoyed with coffee in the afternoon. Wonderful with raspberry jam.

2 eggs
1 cup flour
1 tsp. baking soda
½ cup milk
2 Tbsp. sugar
sour cream

Beat eggs and sugar until thick and well blended. Add flour and baking soda, a little at a time with milk. Add enough sour cream until the batter has the consistency of thick pancake batter.

Grease a medium-hot waffle iron and bake waffles until golden brown. Serve.

God mat og gode venner går bra sammern.

Good food and good friends go well together.

FYRSTEKAKE - PRINCE'S CAKE

A lovely, almond-filled dessert. Makes one cake.

¾ cup butter
½ cup sugar
1 to 2 egg yolks
2 Tbsp. water
½ tsp. baking powder
1¾ cups all-purpose flour

Filling:

1 cup almonds, grated
¾ cup powdered sugar
½ tsp. almond extract

Cream butter and sugar until soft. Mix in egg yolks and water. Line bottom and sides of round, well-greased 9" spring form pan with half of the dough.

Mix together grated almonds, powdered sugar and almond extract. Put into lined pan. On a floured bread board, roll out the other half of dough and, with a sharp knife, cut strips about ¼" to ½" thick. Place the strips over filling in a woven criss-cross pattern.

Bake on lower rack in oven at 375° F for 30 to 40 minutes, or until golden.

AUNT TILLIE'S KRUMKAKER
AUNT TILLIE'S COOKIE ROLLS

Krumkaker is never missing from a Norwegian Christmas party and shows up at most festive occasions. It is often served filled with whipped cream mixed with a bit of berry jam. Makes over a dozen.

2 medium eggs
½ cup sugar
1 cup all-purpose flour
½ cup (1 stick) melted butter or margarine
¼ tsp. almond extract
¼ tsp. vanilla extract

Beat eggs slightly and add sugar and flour. Add the melted butter and flavoring. Drop a tablespoon of the batter into heated Krumkake iron. Bake until golden. Roll the flat cake into a cone while still hot, handle carefully, it is very fragile. Fill if desired when cool.

AUNT TILLIE'S SANDKAKER
AUNT TILLIE'S TARTS

Sandkaker is thought to have originated in Oslo. These cookies are especially popular at Christmas. The cookies pop out easily from the tinforms.

¼ cup sugar
1 cup butter
1 egg
15 almonds, chopped fine
1 Tbsp. almond extract
2½ cups all-purpose flour

Cream sugar and butter. Add egg and rest of ingredients. Press into tinforms. Bake 30 minutes at 350° F or until golden.

FATTIGMANNSBAKKELS
POOR MAN'S COOKIES

A Norwegian favorite, made every Christmas. Makes about a dozen.

3 egg yolks
¼ cup sugar
2 to 3 Tbsp. whipping cream
1 cup all-purpose flour
¼ tsp. cardamom

Beat yolks and sugar together. Whip cream and add it to the yolk mixture. Sift flour together with the cardamom and add to cream mixture. Mix well. Divide the dough into two parts. Roll thin. Cut into diamond shapes. Make a slit in the center of each cookie and draw one corner through so that it will look like a knot. Deep fry the cookies till they are golden brown. May be dusted with powdered sugar.

SERINAKAKER - SERINA COOKIES

Delicate almond-topped cookies. Makes about 60 cookies.

2 cups chilled butter
4 cups all-purpose flour
1½ tsp. baking powder
2 eggs, separated
2 cups sugar
4 tsp. vanilla sugar
½ cup almonds

Cut cold butter into the mixed flour and baking powder. Next add egg yolks and 1 egg white beaten with sugar and vanilla sugar. Make small balls and flatten them slightly with a fork. Brush remaining egg white on them and sprinkle with chopped almonds. Bake until golden brown in moderate oven, (about 375° F), for about 12 minutes.

KARAMELLPUDDING - CARAMEL PUDDING

Old-fashioned caramel tops this Scandinavian favorite. Serves 6.

Caramel Coating:

1 cup sugar

Melt sugar for caramel in skillet over low heat, until light brown. Coat baking dish (8½" x 4½" x 2½") or mold with syrup immediately.

Pudding:

3 cups milk
3 Tbsp. sugar
6 eggs, minus 2 egg whites
1 tsp. vanilla

Bring milk to a boil. Add three tablespoons sugar. Beat eggs and add to milk. Add vanilla. Pour mixture into coated baking disk and bake in oven at 300° F for 40 minutes, or until mixture does not adhere to knife.

When cool, invert on platter, garnish with whipped cream and chopped almonds. Serve with caramel sauce.

Caramel Sauce:

1 cup sugar
1 cup boiling water
½ cup whipping cream, whipped and sweetened

Melt sugar in a skillet until golden, then add boiling water. Stir until the mixture is smooth and free of all lumps. Cool, and before serving, add whipped cream.

SVISKEKOMPOTT - PRUNE COMPOTE

A simple but good recipe that may be served for breakfast, brunch or as a dessert. The Prune Whip variation is especially good as a light dessert. Serves 4 to 6.

½ lb. pitted prunes
1½ to 2 cups water
1/3 cup sugar
dash of lemon juice, optional

Wash prunes and soak overnight in enough water to cover.

Next day, boil the prunes in the water until they are soft. Make a soft puree of the prunes. Add sugar to taste, and a little lemon juice. Serve with whipped cream, or light cream.

Variation: PRUNE WHIP

4 egg whites

Whip until very dry. Carefully fold in the prune puree. Place in a shallow dish and bake in preheated oven at 350° F for about 25 to 30 minutes. Cool. Serve with whipped cream.

Alt godt kommer i små porsjoner.

All good things come in small portions.

FRANSKBRØDPUDDING
PUDDING OF WHITE BREAD

A home-style pudding flavored with lemon, raisins and almonds. Serve plain or with a fruit sauce. Serves 6.

6 to 8 slices white bread
1 cup milk
2/3 cup butter or margarine
3 eggs, separated
1 Tbsp. sugar
½ to 2/3 cup raisins
grated rind of ½ lemon
10 to 15 chopped blanched almonds

Trim crust off white bread. Place trimmed bread into a deep bowl. Pour milk over the bread and soak for about 1 hour. In a casserole, melt butter until golden. Add the soaked bread and stir until all the butter is absorbed. Remove from heat and cool slightly. Add egg yolks, one at a time. Stir well each time. Add sugar, raisins, lemon rind and chopped almonds. Stir well. Fold in the stiffly beaten egg whites.

Pour the batter into a well-greased, ovenproof dish and bake in preheated oven at 375° to 400° F for about 1 hour.

RIS MED TYTTEBÆRSYLTETØY
RICE WITH LINGONBERRIES

A classic dessert with three different serving options. Serves 6.

2 cups water
½ cup long-grained rice
½ cup sugar
½ cup heavy cream, whipped
lingonberries (stirred lingonberry jam)

Bring water to boil in a saucepan, then add the rice. Reduce heat, and let simmer without lid for about 20 minutes. Add sugar, and when the rice is completely cooled, the whipped cream. Carefully fold in the stirred lingonberry jam, until the dessert has a soft, pink color. Do not add too much, as the jam is fairly strong flavored.

Variation: Add the stirred lingonberry jam to whipped cream, carefully folded in, to achieve the same soft, pink color. Serve immediately.

Variation: In a bowl, place the lingonberry jam in the middle, surrounded with the cooked rice (before adding the whipped cream). Serve with whipped cream separately, or with a light cream poured over individual servings, as much as one would like.

Man skal ikke rette baker for smed.

Do not sentence the baker for the wrong of the blacksmith.

RØMMEGRØT - SWEET CREAMPORRIDGE

This recipe brings back memories and the traditions of Norwegion life; as it was served after bringing the hay in on the farm or when visiting a new mother. Today it is served at parties as a dessert. Serve with melted butter, cinnamon and sugar. Delicious, but beware of the calories! Serves 6 to 8.

4 cups sweet cream
2 cups flour
4 cups milk, scalded
1 tsp. salt
½ cup sugar

Put cream in heavy saucepan and boil for 10 minutes. Sift flour into cream very gradually to prevent lumps from forming. Continue cooking over moderate heat, stirring to bring out butter fat. Remove butter as soon as it forms and put into small pan to keep warm. Add a little more flour to the porridge and when well mixed, add scalded milk, gradually stirring until mixture is smooth. Add salt and sugar and cook about 10 minutes more.

Han går som katten om den varme grøten.

He circles around the warm porridge like a cat.

TYTTEBÆRSYLTETØY - LINGONBERRY JAM

Lingonberries are a Norwegian favorite, but other berries may be substituted.

4½ to 5 qts. berries
5 lbs. sugar
1 vanilla bean
1 lb. peeled and chopped apples

Place the cleaned berries and the sugar in layers in the pan, add the vanilla. Use low heat. When the sugar has melted, add apples. Let boil till the apples are soft, and pour the jam into warm dry jars, removing vanilla bean.

RØRT TYTTEBÆRSYLTETOY
STIRRED LINGONBERRY JAM

This is an old-fashioned Norwegian jam recipe.

4½ to 5 qts. berries
5 lbs. sugar

Stir the cleaned berries with the sugar, (tradition says it should be in one direction), for about 2 hours. Keep the jam in a large covered jar. When some jam is removed from jar, stir remainder a few times.

KÅLRULETTER - CABBAGE ROLLS

Norwegian-style cabbage rolls make a delicious entreé. Serves 4 to 6.

1 medium-sized cabbage
1 lb. ground meat, beef, pork or half each
2 potatoes
1 cup milk
salt, pepper
dry bread crumbs

Place cabbage in boiling, salted water and cook until the leaves are soft. Cook and mash the potatoes; mix well with ground meat. Add bread crumbs, salt, pepper and milk. Put one tablespoon of the ground meat mixture on each cabbage leaf and roll together like a parcel. Tie a bit of thread around each. Boil or fry them.

BOILED: Boil for 30 minutes. Serve with white or brown sauce.

FRIED: Fry in a frying pan. Add the cabbage water and let simmer for 35 minutes. Serve in brown sauce with boiled potatoes and lingonberry jam.

Note: Brown sauce is made from the juices in the pan that is thickened with flour. A color enhancer, such as Kitchen Bouquet, may be added for color.

Fingrene av fatet! - Hands off the dish!

KJØTT I KÅL - FILLED CABBAGE

Cut the cabbage head in wedges before serving. Serve with boiled potatoes and sweet-sour cream sauce. Serves 4 to 6.

1 head cabbage
1 lb. ground beef
½ lb. fresh, ground pork
milk
1 cup bread crumbs
1 egg, beaten
salt, pepper to taste

Slice off top of cabbage head and remove center, leaving about an inch wall of cabbage. Combine meat, bread crumbs, egg and spices. Beat well with enough milk to make the dough fluffy. Fill cabbage. Put the top of cabbage head back to cover the meat. Tie together. Fill a kettle with water, add a little salt, then place the cabbage head in center, surrounded by the cabbage pieces removed from the center. Bring to boil and simmer for about two hours.

Cream Sauce:

3 Tbsp. butter or margarine
4 Tbsp. flour
1 cup liquid from the cabbage broth
1 cup light cream
2 Tbsp. vinegar
3 Tbsp. sugar

Melt butter, stir in flour. Add liquid a little at a time. Bring to a boil. Add vinegar and sugar. Add a little more liquid if the gravy is too thick. Serve in a gravy boat.

SYLTEFLÆSK - HEAD CHEESE

Make your own Scandinavian Head Cheese with this classic recipe.
Makes about a 2 pound pressed loaf.

½ pork head meat and pork rind (meat can be from the shoulder)
¼ lb. veal meat
2 to 3 envelopes unflavored gelatin
2 to 3 tsp. salt
½ tsp. pepper
¼ tsp. cloves
¼ tsp. ginger
¼ tsp. allspice

Cook the pork meat with the rind and veal for 1 hour in salted water. (For 1 quart water, use 1 teaspoon salt.) Remove the rind. Cook the meat for another 1½ hours. Add rind to stock to keep it warm. Cut the meat into thin "sticks" lengthwise. Dip a piece of cheese cloth in warm water and wring it out, place this in a shallow dish. Place the rind on the cloth, rind side down, and place meat and fat in layers with the gelatin and the spices. Put the rest of the rind on top, and wrap the cloth tightly around the head cheese. Sew together or use strong nylon wrapping-string and tie it around the "cheese." Cook the head cheese in the stock for another ½ hour. Remove and put it under press right away, and place in refrigerator until the next day.

Next day, put the head cheese into a brine. Leave the cloth on and leave it in the brine for 8 days. If the cheese should be too salty, soak overnight in cold water.

Brine:

4½ to 5 cups water
5 cups rock salt
1 tsp. saltpeter
½ cup sugar

Put everything in a pot and cook for approximately 5 to 10 minutes. Skim foam off the top. Let cool completely and put the "cheese" in.

FÅR I KÅL - MUTTON AND CABBAGE

A popular dish from southern Norway. Serve with boiled potatoes. Serves 4.

4 lbs. cabbage
2 lbs. mutton
1 Tbsp. whole black pepper

Cut cabbage into quarters and remove the stem. Cut meat into serving pieces, and layer in a heavy pot with the cabbage. Add water so it covers half the meat and cabbage. Add pepper. Cook covered slowly for 3 hours. Test for tenderness. Stir a couple of times and add salt to taste.

Smak og behag kan ikke diskuteres.

Tastes and preferences are not easily discussed.

KLIPPFISK I HVIT SAUS - CREAMED CODFISH

Klippfisk is sundried cod from Northern Norway. For centuries it has been exported to many countries in Europe. It is usually served with boiled potatoes for lunch or dinner. Serves 2 to 3.

1 cup shredded codfish (dried, salted cod)
1 egg
salt and pepper
2 Tbsp. butter
2 Tbsp. all-purpose flour
1 cup milk

Soak fish in cold water overnight. Drain. Add water and heat to boiling point, then drain. Make a white sauce of butter, flour, and milk, add beaten egg gradually. Add codfish and cook 2 minutes.

Uten mat og drikke duger helten ikke.

Without food and drink the hero can do nothing.

LUTEFISK I - LUTEFISH I

Lutefisk is served at Christmas in parts of Norway and Sweden. It is a spring-ling, a cod fish variety which has been lime-cured. Lutefisk can be obtained in Scandinavian delicatessens in the Christmas season. Lutefisk and Lefse are sure foods to bring Norwegians together - while often repelling others!

Allow one pound per person. Soak lutefish in cold water for 3 to 4 hours before using. Remove dark skin and fins, and cut in serving size pieces. Place in cheese cloth and put into a kettle of cold water to which salt has been added. Bring to a boil. Cook about 5 minutes until fish is tender, then drain and serve with drawn butter or a cream sauce.

Variation: Try a little prepared mustard with lutefisk and butter.

LUTEFISK II - LUTEFISH II

This version uses ready to cook lutefisk. Serves 2 to 3.

3 lb. lutefish, ready to cook
1 Tbsp. butter
1 Tbsp. salt
allspice, to taste

Place lutefish skin side down on buttered baking dish. Sprinkle with salt. Cover with aluminum foil and bake in moderate oven, (350° F) for 30 to 40 minutes. Baking time will depend upon the thickness of the fish.

Pour off water before serving. Remove foil and serve with white sauce, melted butter or mustard.

RØKELAKS - SMOKED SALMON

Make your own smoked salmon in the Norwegian tradition. Smoked salmon should not be kept in a refrigerator, which adds too much moisture. Rather, keep it in a dry, cool room, and wrap it in parchment paper.

16 to 18 lbs. salmon
1 qt. salt
1 cup sugar
1 tsp. saltpeter
¼ cup cognac (brandy)

Open salmon along the backbone after head and tail have been cut off. During the cutting the knife should go along the underside of the backbone. Afterwards, the backbone is cut off from the other side. The fish must be cleaned and the blood dried off with a dry rag. Do not use water.

A thick layer of salt and sugar is put on a wooden cutting board. Put the skin side of the salmon down, cover it completely with salt and sugar, and put another wooden board on top. Put some pressure on it the next day. The salmon stays this way for about 60 hours, all the time covered with salt and sugar. Then the salt and sugar are dried off with a piece of cloth, and finally washed over with the saltpeter, dissolved in the cognac. On the skin side, the salmon is widened by means of two wooden splints. The salmon then is smoked for 8 hours in cold smoke. (Most people send it away for smoking.)

After 6 days, it is ready to be served. Keep the salmon lying, not hanging, so that it will not become dry.

Tip: To make salmon broth - Place backbone in cold water with salt. After the water has come to the point of boiling, skim it and add the head and tail. Simmer until done; strain.

FISKEBOLLER - LARGE FISH BALLS

Sailors used to call these Stavanger eggs due partly to the fact that they were for years canned in Stavanger, Norway. The fish balls may be fried in butter after boiling. Serve with fried or boiled potatoes for lunch. For a classic Norwegian meal add carrots, melted butter and bacon bits for a main dish. Also excellent served with steamed carrots in a white sauce. Top with chopped parsley just before serving. Serves 4.

1 lb. fish (haddock or red snapper), deboned
2 to 3 peeled raw potatoes
1 Tbsp. salt, or enough to taste
flour as needed

Cut the ingredients in small pieces; grind or finely chop. Then beat the dough well with coarsely ground white flour, enough flour to make the dough stick when you make large round balls in your hands. Cook in a large pot of salted water. Cook approximately 30 minutes.

SILDESALAT - HERRING SALAD

If you like to make the salad lighter in texture, fold in sour cream, or whipped cream, just before serving. Serves 2 to 3.

1 cup salted herring, cut into small pieces
1 cup pickled beets, diced
1 apple, peeled, cored and chopped into small pieces
1 boiled potato, peeled, cut into small pieces, optional
dash dry mustard
salt and pepper to taste
2 hardboiled eggs

Mix all the ingredients and add mayonnaise, enough to hold the salad together. Add dash of dry mustard, salt and pepper to taste. Decorate with hardboiled eggs, cut into wedges.

FISKESUPPE - FISH SOUP

Serve before lunch, dinner or as an entreé. Soup may be seasoned with a dash of nutmeg. Quantity is flexible depending upon amount of fish added.

Fish (usually cod or any related white fish, such as
  halibut)
3 qts. water
1/3 cup vinegar
1 onion, finely chopped
1 cup shredded carrots
cornstarch
1 cup sour cream
sugar
dash of nutmeg, optional

Clean fish and cut into serving pieces. Boil fish, onion & carrots in water and vinegar. Cook until fish is done. Remove fish from liquid. Thicken soup slightly with cornstarch. Stir until smooth. Return fish pieces to thickened soup. Top with sour cream, a little sugar and nutmeg if desired.

Magan blir mette før øyet.

The stomach is filled before the eye is.

MØLJE - BROTH WITH FLAT BREAD

A very old main dish soup recipe that is a favorite in Northern Norway.

Select a rich, fatty beef bone. Crack the bone to get the benefit of the marrow flavor. Cook in salted water until done, then skim off fat. Pour broth over flat bread, broken into small pieces, and serve piping hot in individual dishes.

En fugl i hånden er bedre enn ti på taket.

One bird in the hand is better than ten on the roof.

BLOMKÅLSUPPE - CAULIFLOWER SOUP

A traditional winter soup, rich and warming. Makes 6 servings.

1 small cauliflower
6 cups water
2 Tbsp. butter
4 Tbsp. all-purpose flour
½ cup cream or half and half
1 egg yolk, beaten
dash of salt
dash of pepper

Cut cauliflower into small pieces. Put into saucepan with 6 cups of water. Cook until tender.

In a saucepan, make sauce with butter, flour and the water from the cauliflower. Add cream, and if necessary, more water to adjust consistancy. Stir in egg yolk. Add salt and pepper to taste. Add cauliflower, heat carefully. Do not boil after adding egg yolk. Serve immediately.

MORMORS SØTSUPPE
GRANDMOTHERS FRUIT SOUP

This fruit soup was made by my grandmother on the farm in Jæren in the southwestern part of Norway. I remember enjoying it after spending all day out in the field gathering in the hay for winter.

½ cup red currants or
½ cup raisins
1 raw apple, cut up
2 cups sugar or to taste
5 cups cold water
1 large cinnamon stick
3 Tbsp. cornstarch

Boil fruit with sugar, water and cinnamon stick until fruit is soft. Add cornstarch, diluted in cold water. Bring back to boil and boil until clear and thick. Serve warm or cold.

TRONDHJEMSUPPE - TRONDHJEM SOUP

Named for a city, this soup may be served before dinner, as an entreé, or as a dessert. Serves 6.

¼ cup rice
6 cups water
¾ cup raisins
juice of 1 lemon
sugar to taste
¼ cup cream
2 egg yolks, beaten

Add rice to boiling water, then add raisins. Cook until well done. Add lemon juice, sugar and cream, which have been well blended. Add beaten egg yolks gradually. Remove from stove. Do not continue cooking after adding egg yolks.

LAPSKAUS - MEAT STEW

A popular dish during World War II. Traditional in some areas as a luncheon dish on May 17th. Usually served with Flatbread. Serves 4.

1 lb. fresh beef
1 lb. fresh pork
1 medium onion, sliced
4 raw potatoes, diced
2 carrots, sliced (optional)
salt and pepper

Dice meat, cover with water and simmer one hour. When meat is tender, add vegetables. Season with salt and pepper. Cook until vegetables are done and stew has thickened.

Mange kokker gjør mye søl.

Many cooks make a mess.

KOMLE - POTATO DUMPLINGS

This classic Norwegion recipe has many names. It is called "Komle" on the West coast, "Kumpe" on the Southern coast, "Raspeball" in Bergen and "Klubb" in Oslo. Served with melted butter. Serves 6.

4 cups grated raw potatoes
½ lb. salt pork or lamb
beef broth
1 tsp. baking powder, (optional)
1 tsp. salt
1 cup all-purpose flour
1 cup graham flour

Dice meat. Mix all ingredients except meat. Shape into balls, put pieces of meat in the center. Add enough flour to keep them from sticking to hands. Drop into boiling broth, cover and boil one hour. Stir occasionally to prevent from sticking. Remove from broth as soon as done.

Tip: Leftover Komle can be cut into halves and fried or sautced for dinner the next day. Often served with berry jam.

RASPEBALLER - POTATO DUMPLINGS

A meatless variation of Potato Dumplings. This version is often served with Split Pea Soup. Serves 6.

4 large potatoes, peeled and grated
1 egg, well beaten
1 Tbsp. butter
salt
flour as needed
broth*

Combine all ingredients. Thicken with flour as necessary. Drop spoonfuls into broth and boil 25 minutes.

*Tip: Ham or pork broth is a Norwegian preference.

BLOMKÅLPUDDING
CAULIFLOWER AU GRATIN

Traditionally served with white sauce. Shrimp or mushrooms are delicious added to the sauce. Serves 4.

4 to 6 eggs, separated
½ cup butter
2/3 cup all-purpose flour
2 cups milk
1 cauliflower, trimmed and boiled
1 tsp. salt
cracker crumbs, amount to taste

Whip egg whites, set aside. Melt the butter, stir in the flour, and little by little add the milk. Let boil for 3 minutes, cool it off, stir into it the egg yolks one at a time, add the salt, finally, add the whipped egg whites. Pour into a buttered and floured glass dish. Alternate with layers of boiled cauliflower. Sprinkle cracker crumbs over top. Put the dish in a pan filled with water. Heat the oven to about 400° F, bake for one hour.

GLASERTE GULERØTTER - GLAZED CARROTS

Carrots, cabbage and root vegetables were the only vegetables available in the winter months in Scandinavia. Today the wonderful diversity of recipes for these vegetables are prepared by choice. Serves 8.

4 cups carrots, scraped, rinsed, and cut into 2 to 4 slices
lengthwise
1 tsp. salt
¼ cup butter or margarine
2 Tbsp. sugar
2 cups water

Put the carrots into a saucepan, pour boiling water over. Add salt, sugar and butter. Cover saucepan and let the carrots boil, until they are fairly soft and the water has almost evaporated. Remove lid and shake the carrots until they look evenly glazed.

SURKÅL - SWEET & SOUR CABBAGE

This is served with any kind of pork dish. Serves 8.

1 large head of cabbage
2 Tbsp. butter
1½ tsp. caraway seed
1 Tbsp. flour
1 tsp. salt
2 cups water or meat stock
1 tsp. vinegar
1 tsp. sugar

Remove the heavy core in cabbage. Shred cabbage into fine strips. In a kettle, add cabbage, butter, flour, salt and caraway seeds. Then add the stock or water. Cover, boil for 1½ hours, stirring frequently. Don't let it boil dry. Before serving, add vinegar and sugar to taste and stir well.

KOKT PURRE MED SMELTET SMØR
BOILED LEEKS WITH MELTED BUTTER

Leeks may be served with fried meatcakes or as a first course for dinner. Serve one leek per person.

1 bunch leeks
water to cover
salt to taste
melted butter

Wash leeks well and trim the roots and upper part of the leaves. Boil leeks until soft in salted water; about 30 minutes. Melt butter and serve it with leeks.

Tiden går fort i godt selskap.

In good company time passes quickly.

SWEDEN

SWEDEN

Best known of Sweden's culinary traditions is the Smörgåsbord, a spectacular collection of delicacies offered buffet style on a decorated table. This contribution to the world's cuisine is said to have originated among the country people of Sweden over two hundred years ago and has gradually attained the reputation of an artistic gastronomical feast. Starting with the customary varieties of herring, the Swedes may add one or two canapes and a bit of potato with bread and butter. A new plate is taken for the egg dishes, salads, cold meats, and aspic. Widely proclaimed Köttbullar (Swedish meat balls) are made of carefully selected and freshly ground meats and served either hot or cold. For a fancy dinner, you will find a starter of three canapes set at each place, not served with a smörgåsbord.

As in all the Scandinavian countries, fish is varied and plentiful, including salmon, eel, herring, cod, trout, flounder, halibut, and shellfish. The Swedish cooks devise numerous original ways of baking, grilling, frying, or boiling fish or combining them into flavorful dishes. Dill and fennel are favorite seasonings.

Special holidays in Sweden call for traditional dishes. At Christmas time, in a ceremony called "dopp i grytan", a special Limpa bread is dipped in the broth used to boil the ham, a ceremony that dates back to pagan feasts, supposedly to bring back the sunlight of spring. As in the other Scandinavian countries, an almond is placed in the holiday rice pudding. In Sweden, each person offered a portion makes up a rhyme before passing the dish along. And the one finding the almond may be married within the year. Smaländsk ostkaka (a special cheesecake) served with lingonberries, is also a Christmas treat in some parts of Sweden.

Salt salmon is the customary entree on Good Friday, and roast lamb on Easter Eve. St. Martin's Day, November 10, is celebrated in southern Sweden, as it is in Denmark, with roast goose stuffed with apples and prunes ... in a tribute to Bishop Martin of Tours, patron saint of innkeepers.

Good use is made of the country's fine dairy products, and pure butter and rich cream make flaky pastries, cream puddings, and crisp cookies. A delicious torte and sju sorters kakor (seven kinds of cookies) are traditionally served for a kaffe kalas (afternoon coffee). When you are invited to a dinner prepared by a Swedish housewife, you may expect unusual fare -- aromatic Nypon soppa (Rose Hip soup) found only in Sweden.

INLAGD SILL - PICKLED HERRING

PICKLED HERRING is always found on a smörgåsbord and there are many different recipes. If you cannot find salt herring, you may buy a jar of "wine herring" from the grocery store. Drain and rinse and make your own "marinade" using the following recipe. Pickled herring with boiled potatoes and hardtack is a typical appetizer at many dinners. Beer and aquavit are served with it.

4 salt herring fillets
½ cup vinegar
1 cup water
¾ cup sugar
1 small red onion, thinly sliced
1 small carrot, thinly sliced
10 crushed allspice
4 bay leaves

Soak herring overnight in cold water.

Mix vinegar, water and sugar in a sauce pan; bring to a boil. Let cool.

Cut herring into serving pieces of approximately ½". Layer in glass jar with onion, carrots, allspice and bay leaves. Pour cold vinegar mixture over herring. Refrigerate 1 to 2 days.

144

PRINS BERTILS PANNKAKOR - PRINCE'S CREPES

Serve two filled crepes per person as an appetizer, 3 to 4 as an entrée.
Leftover, unfilled pancakes freeze well.

3 eggs
1 tsp. salt
1 cup all-purpose flour
4 cups milk or light cream and water, mixed
1 Tbsp. melted butter

Put flour, salt and liquids into bowl and stir until smooth. Let stand for several hours. Add beaten eggs and melted butter. Make thin pancakes, baking one side only and put on a plate, one over the other.

Filling for Crepes:

½ lb. salad shrimp
1 to 2 Tbsp. chopped dill
1 cup Hollandaise Sauce

Add shrimp and dill to Hollandaise sauce.

Topping:

1 cup Swiss cheese, shredded
1/2 cup white bread crumbs

Combine topping ingredients.

Put a few tablespoons of filling at the edge of each pancake. Roll up and place on a greased ovenproof platter. Sprinkle with topping. Place in moderate oven until heated through and top is brown. Use broiler to brown if you are afraid the pancakes might dry out.

Ingen är så mätt att han inte kan få ned en plätt.

Nobody is so full he cannot get down another pancake.

ELIZABETHS JULGLÖGG - CHRISTMAS GLÖGG

This is a favorite recipe among the Swedish lodges in Portland. Glögg is served mainly during the winter months. It tastes great after skiing or warms you up after a walk in the snow. Makes 5 to 10 servings.

1 qt. bottle red wine (use a wine that is not too dry or mix
   half burgundy and half port)
½ to ¾ cup sugar (smaller amount if port wine is used)
2 to 3 cinnamon sticks
10 whole cloves
1 tsp. cardamom seeds, optional
peel from 1 orange
1 to 2 cups brandy or vodka, optional
½ to 1 cup raisins
¼ to ½ cup slivered almonds

In saucepan, combine all ingredients except brandy, raisins or almonds. Heat to simmering, do not boil. Turn off heat; add brandy or vodka if desired. Let stand covered for 2 to 3 days. Strain and pour into bottle. Save raisins for serving time.

Before serving, heat glögg. Serve hot in small glasses or cups with a handle. Add a few raisins and almonds to each cup and serve with a spoon.

DELIKATESSBULLAR - SUPER BUNS

Makes 40 filled buns.

1 pkg. dry yeast
¾ cup milk
¼ cup warm water
2 cups all-purpose flour
2/3 cup butter or margarine at room temperature
½ cup sugar
3 eggs
2 to 3 cups all-purpose flour

Filling:

½ cup butter or margarine
¾ cup sugar
1 tsp. vanilla

Topping:

1 egg, beaten
½ cup slivered almonds

Scald milk to lukewarm. Dissolve yeast in warm water; mix with warm milk. Add 2 cups of flour and beat until smooth. Cover and let rise for 30 minutes.

While dough is rising, beat together filling ingredients. Place 40 paper baking cups on 2 cookie sheets. Using half of filling, put a dab in bottom of each cup.

Work butter, sugar, eggs and rest of flour, a little at a time, into raised dough. Don't overwork. Knead lightly, divide into 40 pieces. Shape each piece into a ball and place in paper baking cup. Cut a slit in each roll and divide rest of filling into each slit.

Cover, let rise 40 to 60 minutes. Brush with beaten egg and sprinkle with almonds. Bake in 400° F oven for 8 to 10 minutes.

LIMPA - SWEDISH RYE BREAD

Fragrant, traditional Swedish rye bread. Makes 3 loaves.

½ cup margarine or shortening
4 cups milk
½ cup brown sugar
½ cup molasses
1 tsp. fennel seeds
1 tsp. anise seeds
2 Tbsp. grated orange peel, optional
2 cups rye flour
1 Tbsp salt
1 package dry yeast
8 cups white flour, approximately

Combine margarine, milk, brown sugar, molasses, anise, fennel and orange peel in a large saucepan. Heat, stirring occasionally until margarine is melted. Add rye flour and salt. Continue to stir until heated. Set aside to cool slightly.

Dissolve yeast in small amount of warm water. Pour rye mixture into large mixing bowl; add yeast mixture. Gradually add white flour until dough pulls away from the sides. Lightly oil top of dough, cover and let rise until doubled in size.

Turn dough onto floured baking board. Divide into 3 parts. Knead and shape each part into a loaf. Place in greased loaf pans. Cover and let rise until doubled in size.

Bake in a 325° F oven for 45 to 60 minutes. Tops may be brushed with melted butter, if desired. Cool on rack.

Spisat bröd är snart glömt. Eaten bread is soon forgotten.

TUNNA PANNKAKOR - SWEDISH PANCAKES

Pancakes are a famous Swedish dish traditionally served as dessert after a soup dinner, especially on Thursdays when pea soup is served. Makes 4 servings.

2 eggs
1 Tbsp. sugar
1 Tbsp. butter or margarine, melted and cooled
¾ cup buttermilk
1 cup flour
1 tsp. lemon peel or grated lemon rind
1 tsp. cardamom
1¼ to 11/3 cups milk

Whip eggs with sugar, then add the melted, cooled butter. Add buttermilk and stir well. Mix flour with spices. Add to the egg mixture, alternating with the milk. Whip until smooth. Batter should be thin.

Melt a little shortening on a medium-hot omelet pan, covering thoroughly. Add a ladlespoon of batter. Rotate the pan to spread the batter in a thin layer. When cooking side is golden brown, turn to cook other side. (Batter will be transparent looking when ready to be turned.) Serve warm, rolled up with jam, whipped cream or other delicious fillings.

Lätt som en plätt. - Easy as a pancake.

KRÄMOST, FÄRSKOST - FRESH CHEESE

There are many variations to this recipe. In northern Sweden and Norway, goat's milk is often substituted for cow's milk.

4 qts. fresh, whole pasteurized milk
1 qt. cultured buttermilk

Heat whole milk to a little more than finger warmth in a large kettle. Add buttermilk and stir very well. Cover. Heat oven to "warm" and place the milk mixture in the oven for 8 to 12 hours. The mixture is ready to come out of the oven when the milk mix is well set. For a more sour taste, leave the milk in the oven a bit longer.

Put the kettle on low heat. Gradually increase the heat, stirring gently. When the milk has started to curdle, remove from heat, cover and cool.

Line a large colander with cheese cloth. Spoon cooled curds into the lined colander and let drip until fairly dry (in the refrigerator, if possible). This will take several hours, perhaps overnight.

Tip curds into a bowl and work with a spoon until smooth.

KRÄMOST (served for dessert):

Mix the cheese with ½ cup heavy cream, whipped, and form into a ball. Place on a pretty platter and pipe whipped cream around it. Serve with berries or cinnamon and sugar.

KRÄMOST (served for smörgåsbord):

Add salt and chopped chives or cumin to the cheese. Adjust flavoring to taste.

FÄRSKOST:

Add two eggs to the curdled milk and whisk the mixture while heating. The mixture should not boil. Take off heat and let stand until whey is clear. Process according to directions above. Press curds into a decorative pan, tip out onto an ovenproof platter, brush with melted butter and bake until lightly browned. Serve with the smörgåsbord.

NOTE: LEFTOVER WHEY:

Leftover whey can be used as a liquid in bread. It is especially good in rye bread. It can also be used to make Whey Butter.

Ost och bröd gör kinden röd.

Cheese and bread, make the cheek red.

MESSMÖR - WHEY BUTTER

WHEY BUTTER is made with leftover whey. It is a very traditional spread in central and northern Sweden.

Boil down leftover whey to a caramel colored mass, the consistency of thick honey. This takes several hours and needs watching and stirring, especially in the later stages. When the desired consistency is reached, cool and whip with a few tablespoons of butter.

Gå åt som smör i solsken.

Run out like butter in sunshine.

TOSCA TÅRTA - ALMOND-TOPPED CAKE

An easy and quick one-layer cake. Makes one cake.

2 eggs
2/3 cup sugar
1 cup flour
1 tsp. baking powder
4 oz. butter or margarine, melted
2 Tbsp. milk or cream

Topping:

½ cup sliced almonds
2 oz. butter or margarine
1/3 cup sugar
1 Tbsp. flour
1 Tbsp. milk or cream

Grease and flour (or use breadcrumbs) an 8 to 9 inch cake pan.

Beat eggs and sugar. Mix flour and baking powder; add to egg mixture. Stir in melted butter and milk. Pour into cake pan. Bake in 350° F oven for 20 minutes, until barely done.

While cake is baking, make topping. Mix all ingredients in sauce pan. Heat while stirring. Take off heat when mixture reaches a boil. Spread topping over cake and finish baking for 10 more minutes or until topping is golden brown. Cool. To remove from pan, invert onto waxed paper lined pan. Quickly invert onto serving plate.

RULLTÅRTA - JELLY ROLL

This is the classic Scandinavian Jelly Roll. Makes one cake roll.

3 eggs
½ cup sugar
¾ cup flour
1 tsp. baking powder
3 Tbsp. milk

Filling:

¾ cup jam, jelly or applesauce

Beat eggs and sugar until light and fluffy. Mix flour and baking powder. Carefully stir flour and milk into egg mixture.

Pour batter into greased jellyroll pan (pan may be lined with greased aluminimum foil or waxed paper). Bake in 375° to 400° F oven for about 5 minutes. Watch carefully, the cake burns easily.

When done, immediately turn onto towel (remove foil or waxed paper if used). Sprinkle with sugar. Working quickly, spread with jam. Roll cake tightly in towel. Cool on wire rack.

Variation: BAKELSER - JELLY TARTS Makes about 15 slices. Slice jelly roll. Top each slice with whipped cream and jam or fruit such as apricot halves, strawberries or mandarin oranges.

SKÅNSK ÄPPELKAKA
APPLECAKE FROM SKÅNE

This is the dessert traditionally served on St. Martin's Day, November 11, in Skåne, Sweden's most southern province, as well as in Denmark. Serve with Vanilla Sauce. Makes 6 generous servings.

4 Tbsp. butter
1 1/3 cups tart, thick applesauce
2 cups bread crumbs, white, wheat or pumpernickel
2 Tbsp. butter

Melt butter in skillet. Lightly brown crumbs in butter. Put a third of the crumbs in a buttered cake pan, top with half of the applesauce, add a third of the bread crumbs and remaining applesauce, top with remaining crumbs. Smooth top and dot with remaining butter.

Bake in 400° F oven for 25 to 30 minutes. Cool, unmold. Sprinkle with powdered sugar. For an attractively decorated cake, cut a snowflake from a round piece of wax paper. Place the snowflake on top of the cake and sprinkle with powdered sugar.

VANILJSÅS - VANILLA SAUCE

Excellent served over Applecake as well as other desserts. If available, cook in a double boiler. Serves 6.

1¼ cups light cream or milk
2 egg yolks or 1 egg
1½ tsp. cornstarch
2 Tbsp. sugar
2 tsp. vanilla
¾ to 1 cup heavy cream, whipped

Scald cream. Mix sugar, egg yolks and cornstarch in a heavy saucepan. Add hot cream and whisk. Cook gently until thick, stirring constantly. Remove from heat and whisk until cooled. Add vanilla. Cool in refrigerator. Fold in whipped cream before serving.

HERRGÅRDSTÅRTA - MANORHOUSE CAKE

This well-loved Swedish cake recipe is also called a GLÖMMINGETÅRTA. Decorate with berries. Makes one cake.

Cake:

1 cup (2 sticks) butter or margarine
¾ cup sugar
4 egg yolks
1¼ cups all-purpose flour
3 tsp. baking powder
2/3 cup milk

Meringue:

4 egg whites
1¼ cup sugar
2 tsp. vanilla
almond slivers, to taste

Filling:

1¼ cup whipping cream
berries, fruit, if desired

Cake: Cream butter and sugar until light and fluffy. Add egg yolks, one at a time. Mix flour and baking powder and add alternately with milk to mixture. Beat well. Spread batter in well-greased and floured jelly roll pan.

Meringue: Beat egg whites until stiff. Fold in sugar, vanilla and half of almonds. Spread meringue on top of cake batter. Sprinkle remaining almonds on top. Bake in preheated oven, 350° F for about 20 minutes. Cover cake if meringue gets too dark.

Cool, divide cake in half. Whip cream. Fresh or frozen berries may be mixed with the cream. Spread cake with cream, put one half on top of the other. Tidy up edges. Chill until ready to serve.

SMÅLÄNDSK OSTKAKA
SWEDISH CHEESECAKE FROM SMÅLAND

Serve this uniquely Swedish cheesecake warm with lingonberries, strawberry jam or other fruits and whipped cream. Makes one cheesecake.

2 cups cottage cheese
¼ cup all-purpose flour
3 eggs
¼ cup sugar
2 cups light or heavy cream
¼ to ½ cup blanched, chopped almonds

Beat cottage cheese with electric mixer until smooth. Add all remaining ingredients; mix well. Pour mixture into greased baking pan. Bake in a 350° F oven 1 hour or until set.

Inte vara värd ett ruttet lingon.

Not to be worth a rotten lingonberry.

MANDELFORMAR - ALMOND TARTS

Almond tarts are delicious eaten plain as a cookie. They may also be filled with whipped cream, fruit or jam and served as dessert. Often served on Christmas Eve in western Sweden. Makes 35 to 45 tarts.

1½ sticks butter or margarine
¾ cup sugar
1 egg
1¾ cups all-purpose flour
½ cup blanched, ground almonds

Cream butter and sugar. Add egg, flour and ground almonds. Let rest in refrigerator for 1 hour.

Butter tartlet tins (small round tins with ruffled edges) and press dough inside, just to the rim. Bake in 375° F oven for 10 to 12 minutes or until light golden brown. Cool slightly and invert to remove from tin.

Note: To avoid soggyness, fill just before serving.

Vägen till mannens hjärta går genom magen.

The way to a man's heart is through his stomach.

TANT HARRIETS PEPPARKAKOR
AUNT HARRIET'S GINGER SNAPS

Classic and fragrant Scandinavian Ginger Snaps are a holiday must!

1½ sticks butter or margarine
1½ cups sugar
1/3 cup sorghum or molasses or dark syrup
1 cup water
1 Tbsp. ground ginger
1 Tbsp. cinnamon
1 Tbsp. cloves
2 tsp. crushed cardamom seeds
1 Tbsp. baking soda
7 to 8 cups all-purpose flour

Cream butter and sugar until light and fluffy. Stir in syrup and water. Beat. Add spices and soda. Add flour, reserving about 2 cups. Refrigerate overnight. Roll out thinly, using extra flour as needed; use cookie cutters to cut into desired shapes. Bake in moderate, 350° F oven about 8 minutes or until done.

DRÖMMAR - DREAM COOKIES

Light and melting butter cookies.

1 cup (2 sticks) butter or margarine
¾ cups sugar
2 tsp. vanilla
2 cups all-purpose flour
1 tsp. baker's ammonia, or 1 tsp. baking powder

Beat butter, sugar, and vanilla together. Add flour and ammonia or baking powder. Shape into a long roll the thickness of a thumb. Cut into one inch lengths and roll into small balls. Place on ungreased cookie sheet. Bake in 250° F oven 30 minutes or until very light brown.

KNÄCKKAKOR - CARAMEL COOKIES

A rich and wonderful cookie. Golden syrup is available in the gourmet or imported foods sections of most markets.

1 cup sugar
¼ cup golden syrup
¼ cup heavy cream
¾ cup melted butter or margarine
1 cup oats
1 cup all-purpose flour
½ tsp. baking powder
1 tsp. vanilla

Mix all ingredients. Drop heaping teaspoons of dough onto well-greased cookie sheet. Dough will spread, so place far apart. Bake in 350° F oven until well browned around edges. Remove from oven and let rest for a few minutes. Shape over a rolling pin or a bottle. Cool.

Variation: Cool flat and spread chocolate butter-cream between two cookies.

Chocolate Butter-Cream:

¼ cup (½ stick) butter or margarine
1 Tbsp. cocoa
1 Tbsp. powdered sugar

Beat all ingredients together until light and fluffy.

Låt maten tysta mun. - Let the food silence your mouth.

SMÅ SOCKERSKORPOR, JÄSTPULVERSKORPOR
SMALL SUGAR-RUSKS

These rusks are traditionally served with fruit compotes and
berry soups, or with tea and coffee. Makes about 100.

½ cup butter or margarine
1/3 cup sugar
1 egg
2 cups all-purpose flour
2 tsp. baking powder
1 tsp. crushed cardamom seeds
¼ cup cream

Preheat oven to 350° F. Cream butter and sugar until light. Add egg;
beat. Add flour mixed with baking powder, alternately with cream.
Mix lightly as for biscuits. Pat or roll out to
½" thickness. Cut tiny rounds, about 1" diameter. Put on ungreased
cookie sheet and bake immediately, until very lightly browned.

Take out of oven, split rusk with fork. Return to oven, and
lightly toast cut surface. Let rusk dry in oven (turn off heat).

BÄRSOPPA - BERRY SOUP

In Sweden, this soup is made ahead and served chilled for dessert with cookies. Makes 6 servings.

4 cups fresh or frozen blueberries, strawberries or other fruits   or berries
1½ qts. cold water
½ to 2/3 cup sugar
lemon to taste (if you use fresh, 1 to 2 slices)
1 whole cinnamon stick
3 Tbsp. potato starch
¼ cup cold water

In a large saucepan, bring water, berries, lemon, sugar and cinnamon stick to a boil over medium heat. Simmer over low heat until fruit is soft (approximately 10 to 20 minutes). Mix potato starch with ¼ cup cold water. Add mixture, stirring constantly until thickened and clear. Immediately remove from heat. Let cool covered.

KNÄCK - SWEDISH TOFFEE

This hard candy is a traditional Christmas treat in Sweden. Makes about 60 pieces.

1 cup heavy cream
1 cup dark corn syrup
1 cup sugar
½ cup finely chopped almonds
(4 Tbsp. bread crumbs)
(1/8 tsp. baking powder)

Mix cream, syrup and sugar in a heavy saucepan. Cook to hard ball stage, about 25 minutes (248° F on candy thermometer). Pour a little bit into cold water. If you can roll it, the knäck is done. Mix in chopped almonds. (The bread crumbs and baking powder can now be added to extend the recipe, the baking powder makes the knäck more porous.) Put a teaspoonful of Knäck into little paper cups. Keep in tin with a tight-fitting lid.

APELSINRIS - RICE WITH ORANGES

APELSINRIS is a creamy dessert made with oranges. A similar Swedish dessert is called RIS A LA MALTA, which is made without oranges. Makes 4 servings.

2/3 cup rice
water
3 to 4 oranges
4 Tbsp. sugar
2/3 cup whipping cream
vanilla or vanilla sugar

Cook rice in water according to directions. When done, rinse in cold water. Drain.

Peel and cut oranges into small pieces, reserving some for decorative slices. Sprinkle sugar on oranges pieces. Whip the cream. Add vanilla to taste. Mix rice, oranges and cream just before serving. Garnish with orange slices.

Ta' skeden i vacker hand.

Take the spoon in contented hand.

HOVDESSERT - ROYAL DESSERT

This is a fast, easy and luscious dessert. Ready to serve chocolate sauce may be used if preferred. Makes 4 to 6 servings.

1¼ cups whipping cream
2 Tbsp. sugar
½ tsp. vanilla extract
12 to 16 meringue cookics
¾ cup chocolate sauce

Whip cream; add sugar and vanilla. Place half of meringues on serving plate. Cover with half of whipped cream and half of chocolate sauce. Repeat layering. Garnish with slivered almonds if desired. Serve immediately.

Chocolate sauce:

½ cup cocoa
½ cup extra-fine sugar
dash salt
½ cup water

Mix cocoa, sugar, salt in a saucepan. Add water, blend thoroughly. Over medium heat, warm the cocoa mixture, stirring continuously, until it starts to boil. Let boil for about 1 minute until thickened.

Meringues:

3 egg whites
1¼ cup sugar
a few drops of white vinegar, optional

Beat egg whites with a third of the sugar (and the optional vinegar) until stiff. Fold in the remaining sugar. Place aluminum foil on a cookie sheet (do not butter) and drop the meringue batter by the teaspoonful. (Use a tablespoon to make larger cookies.) In a 225° to 250° F oven, bake the meringues for 35 minutes, until they feel light and can easily be removed from the foil.

KÅLPUDDING - CABBAGE PUDDING

Serve with boiled potatoes, lingonberries and a salad. Serves 4.

½ cup bread crumbs
1 cup milk
1 Tbsp. grated onion
1 tsp. salt
¼ tsp. pepper
1 egg, optional
1 lb. ground beef
2 lbs. cabbage
2 to 4 Tbsp. margarine
brown sugar, optional

Combine bread crumbs, milk, onion, salt, pepper and egg in mixing bowl. Let sit for 15 to 20 minutes. Add ground beef and mix well. If the meat mixture feels thick, add more milk.

Cut cabbage into small pieces and brown lightly in margarine.

Layer cabbage and meat mixture in greased casserole dish, beginning and ending with cabbage. Some brown sugar may be sprinkled over top layer. Bake in 350° F oven for approximately 1 hour.

När det regnar välling har den fattige ingen sked.

When it rains porridge, the poor have no spoons.

PYTTIPANNA - HASH

This is a great dish to use up left-over meats and cooked potatoes. Served with fried eggs and pickled beets. Makes 4 to 6 servings.

2 to 3 Tbsp. butter or margarine
2 yellow or red onions, chopped
2 to 3 cups cooked meat, cut in cubes
7 to 8 boiled potatoes, peeled and diced
1 small Kosher style pickle (saltgurka), diced

Sauté onion in butter until transparent. Add all other ingredients, stirring carefully until potatoes are browned and meat is hot. Season well with salt and pepper.

Den som gapar efter mycket, mister ofta hela stycket.

He who reaches for a lot, often loses all.

KÖTTBULLAR - MEATBALLS

Your favorite seasoning may be added to this basic meatball recipe or substitute pork sausage for the ground pork for a different flavor. Meatballs may be served hot or cold on a smörgåsbord or with gravy and potatoes for dinner. Make gravy by adding water and/or cream to drippings in skillet and thicken with flour. Makes 4 servings.

½ cup dry breadcrumbs
1 cup milk
1 lb. ground beef
¼ lb. ground pork
1 tsp. salt
¼ tsp. pepper
1/3 Tbsp. finely chopped or grated onion
1 egg

Combine breadcrumbs and milk; let stand for 10 minutes. Add remaining ingredients. Mix well and shape into balls.

Brown butter or margarine in skillet. Add a few meatballs at a time and cook, shaking pan to roll balls around until done.

SJÖMANSBIFF - SAILOR'S BEEF

Sprinkle with chopped parsley and serve directly from casserole. Serves 4.

1 lb. boneless beef chuck or round
1½ lbs. potatoes
2 to 3 onions
2 Tbsp. butter or margarine
1 tsp. salt, white pepper
1 to 2 cups beer (or water and sherry)

Cut meat into ½" slices and pound thin. Peel potatoes and onions and cut into thin slices. Brown meat in butter. Place alternate layers of potatoes, meat and onions, each layer sprinkled with salt and pepper, in covered casserole. Deglaze frying pan with a bit of water, pour over casserole. Add beer to just cover, and simmer, covered, for 1 hour or until meat is tender. Or casserole can be baked in the oven for about 1½ hours at 325° F.

PLOMMONSPÄCKAD FLÄSKKARRE
STUFFED PORK ROAST

A classic dish. Serve with roasted or boiled potatoes, vegetables, and thick applesauce. Serves 4.

2 to 3 lbs. pork loin roast
12 pitted prunes
1 tsp. salt
pepper to taste
7 to 10 whole allspice*

Gravy:

2 Tbsp. flour
12/3 cups water or liquid from boiled potatoes or vegetables
heavy cream

Cut the prunes in half. Cut slits in the meat (cut along the muscles) and stuff with the prunes. Rub the meat with salt and pepper (try other spices*, if you wish).

Place the meat, fat side up, in a casserole dish and add the allspice. Cover with aluminum foil and cook in a preheated oven, 350° F, for about 2 to 2½ hours. Take the meat and whole allspice out and set aside. Pour hot water into dish and stir to dissolve the juices. Make gravy by bringing the meat juices, mixed with the hot water, to a boil. Stir the flour with enough water to make a smooth paste, add to the boiling gravy. Stir until the gravy has the consistancy desired. Add salt and pepper to taste, with a little heavy cream, for extra richness. If you are boiling peeled potatoes or vegetables, use the liquid from those instead of water for extra flavor to the gravy.

*Note: Some like to add a bit of ginger, sage and/or rosemary to this dish as well.

TORSK MED MANDEL - COD WITH ALMONDS

A very typical Swedish family recipe usually served with boiled or mashed potatoes and a vegetable. Serves 4.

1½ lbs. cod or other white fish fillets
3 Tbsp. butter or margarine, melted
2 Tbsp. almond slivers
2 Tbsp. bread crumbs
2 Tbsp. grated cheese
salt, pepper to taste
2 to 3 Tbsp. chopped parsley
1 tsp. chervil
1 tsp. tarragon

Place the fish fillets in an ovenproof dish. Brush the top sides of fish with butter, add salt and pepper and sprinkle with almond slivers, bread crumbs, grated cheese and herbs.

Cover with aluminum foil. Bake in 425° F, preheated oven for 15 to 20 minutes. Uncover dish and bake for another 5 to 6 minutes, until fish is golden brown.

Rätta mun efter matsäcken.

Adjust your mouth to the supply.

GRAVLAX - PICKLED SALMON

A classic Swedish dish. Some people like to eat their gravlax with a special sauce. The sauce recipe follows this one. Serves 12.

4 to 4½ lbs. fresh or frozen, thawed salmon (middle piece is best)
¼ cup sugar
¼ cup salt
1 tsp. crushed white pepper
1 large bunch fresh dill

If the salmon is fresh, freeze for 24 hours and then thaw. Scrape and dry salmon, fillet and remove all bones. Leave skin intact. Mix salt, sugar and pepper. Put half of the salmon, skin side down in a glass or china dish, sprinkle with half of the salt mix and half the dill. Place on top ⟩ the other salmon half, thick on thin. Sprinkle with remaining salt mix and dill. Cover and put a weight on top. Refrigerate 24 to 48 hours. (The salmon may be refrigerated in the mix for up to a week.)

When ready, either cut into thick pieces ¾ inches across for a main dish or in very thin, slanted slices for the smörgåsbord or for sandwiches. Decorate the serving plate with fresh dill sprigs and twisted lemon slices.

GRAVLAXSÅS - GRAVLAX SAUCE

Makes 12 servings.

4 Tbsp. mustard
2 Tbsp. sugar
1 egg yolk, optional
4 Tbsp. vinegar
¾ cup oil
chopped dill
salt, pepper, to taste

Mix mustard, sugar, egg yolk and vinegar. Slowly add oil while beating with electric mixer. Sauce should be thick. Add chopped dill and salt and pepper to taste.

RÖDSPÄTTA MED CURRY GRÄDDE
SOLE WITH CURRY SAUCE

An excellent dish that is easy and quick to make. Serve immediately, while the curry sauce slowly melts. Serves 4.

1 cup rice
1 to 1½ lbs. sole or other fish fillets
2 cups water
1½ tsp. salt
½ tsp. curry
½ tsp. dill weed, optional

Sauce:

2/3 cup whipping cream
1 tsp. curry
½ tsp. dill weed, optional
6 oz. cooked shrimp

Place rice in a low, wide, covered baking dish. Put sole fillets on top; add water and spices. Let simmer under cover in a 400° F oven about 25 minutes. Whip the cream and add curry and dill. Pour over fish and rice. Decorate with shrimp.

FISK-OCH SKALDJURSALLAD
FISH AND SHELLFISH SALAD

Also known as WEST COAST SALAD, this mixed seafood salad may be served as an appetizer, light entreé or as a late supper. Good with crusty, french bread. Serves 4 to 8.

1 head lettuce
½ lb. crab meat or imitation crab
½ lb. cooked small shrimps
2 doz. cooked, cleaned mussels (or 1 can, drained)
1 cup frozen peas, thawed
½ lb. mushrooms, sliced
¼ to 1/3 cup Italian salad dressing flavored with 1 clove garlic, crushed

Garnishes:

hardcooked egg slices
asparagus spears
tomato wedges
fresh dill

Place lettuce on a platter or in salad bowl. Combine crab, shrimp, mussels, peas and mushrooms. Add salad dressing; toss. Arrange on top of lettuce. Add garnishes.

Lägg inte alla ägg i samma korg.

Don't put all your eggs in the same basket.

RÖDBETSSALLAD - BEET SALAD

A typical Scandinavian salad that is delicious in either variation.

1½ cups pickled beets, cut into strips
1 apple, coarsley grated
½ cup whipping cream, whipped
horseradish, optional

Carefully mix beets, apple and whipped cream. Season with horseradish if desired. Served chilled with cold meats or fish.

Variation: HERRINGSALLAD - HERRING SALAD is made as above but add chopped salt or wine herring, cooked, cubed potatoes, diced onion and dill pickle. Garnish with chopped, hard-cooked egg.

JORDÄRTSKOCKSSOPPA
CREAM OF JERUSALEM ARTICHOKE SOUP

A lovely and unusual soup. Makes 4 servings.

1 lb. Jerusalem artichokes
1½ Tbsp. butter
3 Tbsp. flour
1½ qts. chicken broth and water from cooking chokes
salt, dash paprika
2 to 3 Tbsp. dry sherry
1 egg yolk
½ cup cream or half and half

Wash chokes and scrape carefully. Slice and place in small amount of lightly salted, boiling water. Cook, covered, until soft. Take out about 1 cup of chokes. Run rest through food processor. Make roux of butter and flour in saucepan. Add hot broth, a little at a time, whisking constantly. Add pureed chokes. Season carefully with salt, paprika and sherry.

Beat yolk and cream together in warmed tureen. Add soup slowly at first, whisking vigorously, pour rest of soup into tureen. Add reserved sliced chokes.

Ju flera kockar dess sämre soppa.

Too many cooks spoil the broth.

NYPONSOPPA - ROSE HIP SOUP

This Swedish soup is high in vitamin C and has been traditionally served in the winter months when fresh fruit was difficult to obtain. Serve cold with whipped cream or vanilla ice cream topped with slivered almonds. Rusks or crushed corn flakes may be used as a topping.

1½ to 2 cups dried rose hips
1½ qts. water
¼ to 1/3 cup sugar
1 Tbsp. potato starch

Rinse rose hips and crush lightly. Place in saucepan with water; bring to a boil and simmer until tender. Puree in blender or food processor. Pureed rose hips should measure 1 to 1¼ quarts, (add water if needed).

Pour puree back into saucepan. Add sugar; stir. Cook mixture over medium heat. Mix potato starch with small amount of water. Slowly stir potato starch liquid into soup. Remove from heat when soup reaches a boil. Chill.

BRUNKÅL - BROWN CABBAGE

Brown cabbage is traditional for Skåne, a province in southern Sweden. It is usually served with ham, sausage or cold meats.

2 lbs. cabbage, shredded
2 to 3 Tbsp. butter or margarine
2 Tbsp. brown sugar
broth or water
salt to taste

In a large saucepan, melt butter and sugar. Add the shredded cabbage. Stir constantly until cabbage is evenly browned. When cabbage is nicely browned, add a little broth or water. Reduce heat and simmer until cabbage is tender. The cabbage may also be cooked with a piece of fresh or salt side of pork.

Tip: Kitchen Bouquet may be added for deeper color.

BRUNA BÖNAR - BROWN BEANS

A traditional Swedish dish that is served with fried salt pork on Tuesdays during Lent and is often found on the Christmas Smörgåsbord in some parts of Sweden. Serves 6.

2 cups dried brown beans
1 to 1½ qts. water
1½ tsp. salt
1/3 cup brown sugar
2 to 3 Tbsp. white vinegar
salt to taste
1 Tbsp. cornstarch mixed with a little cold water

Wash beans, let soak in salted water several hours or overnight. Bring to a boil; reduce heat and simmer until the beans are tender, approximately 1½ hours. If necessary, add more water. When the beans are tender, add sugar, vinegar and salt to taste. Stir in enough of cornstarch mixture to thicken the beans. Serve hot.

BRYNTA KÅLRÖTTER
BROWNED RUTABAGAS (SWEDES)

Good served with beef roast. Makes 4 to 6 servings.

2 rutabagas
3 Tbsp. butter or pan drippings
1 tsp. brown sugar
salt

Peel and slice the rutabagas in ½" slices. Boil in small amount of lightly salted water until almost done. Drain well, and cut into strips or dice. Brown butter or pan drippings in skillet.

Add rutabagas and sprinkle with sugar. Stir, and sauté until evenly browned. Salt lightly.

HELSTEKT GUL LÖK - GLAZED ONIONS

Serve on the Smörgåsbord, or with roast beef, goose or turkey. Serves 6.

6 to 8 small onions, about 1½ lbs.
2 Tbsp. butter
1 tsp. brown sugar
½ cup bouillon

Peel onions. Boil in lightly salted water until almost done, drain. Brown butter in skillet, add onions and sprinkle with sugar. Turn and brown carefully. Add bouillon, cover, and bake in medium oven, (350° - 375° F.), until done, about 30 minutes.

HASSELBACKSPOTATIS
HAZEL HILL POTATOES

Good with roast beef or baked chicken. Serves 6.

12 to 14 small oval potatoes
3 Tbsp. butter, melted
2 tsp. salt
2 to 3 Tbsp. fine, white bread crumbs
4 to 5 Tbsp. grated cheese

Peel potatoes, cut into thin slices crosswise, but not all the way through. Gently pull apart. Place in greased, ovenproof dish, brush generously with melted butter. Bake in hot oven (425° F) for about a half hour. When almost done, brush with more melted butter and sprinkle with salt, bread crumbs and cheese. Bake until done.

JANSSONS FRESTELSE
JANSSON'S TEMPTATION

JANSSONS FRESTELSE is always found on a Swedish smörgåsbord. It is a very popular dish and can also be served as a main dish. Makes 4 to 6 servings.

6 medium potatoes
2 onions
1 can (4 oz.) anchovy fillets
1 cup half and half or heavy cream
2 Tbsp. butter or margarine

Peel potatoes and cut into thin strips. Peel onions and slice thinly. In buttered 2 quart baking dish, layer potatoes, onions and anchovies, ending with potatoes. Pour juice from anchovies and half of cream over potatoes. Dot with butter or margarine and bake in 400° F oven for 45 minutes or until potatoes are tender. Add remaining cream during last part of baking.

GRATINERADE PALSTERNACKOR
PARSNIPS AU GRATIN

Other vegetables can be substituted such as broccoli, cauliflower, leek, Jerusalem artichokes, etc. Makes 6 servings.

1½ lbs. small parsnips
1½ Tbsp. butter
3 Tbsp. flour
2½ to 3 cups half and half
1 egg yolk, beaten
6 Tbsp. parmesan cheese
1 Tbsp. cold butter
dry bread crumbs
grated cheese

Peel parsnips and boil in lightly salted water until done. Slice. Place in well-buttered shallow baking dish. In a saucepan, melt butter, add flour. Slowly add half and half, while stirring. Bring to a boil; boil and stir 3 to 5 minutes until thickened. Add a little sauce to the beaten egg yolk, return all to pan. Add cheese and butter. Do not reheat.

Pour cheese sauce over parsnips. Sprinkle with dry bread crumbs and more cheese. Put under broiler for a few minutes until dish is nicely browned on top.

Komma upp i smöret. - To come up in the butter.

INDEX

183

184

Candies and Cookies

186

Relishes

BOOK ORDER FORM

Culinary Arts Ltd.
P.O. Box 2157, Lake Oswego, OR 97035
(503) 639-4549

☐ **GOURMET MUSTARDS: How To Make And Cook With Them by Helene Sawyer**
ISBN 0-914667-07-6 $ 4.95

☐ **GOURMET VINEGARS: How To Make And Cook With Them by Marsha Peters Johnson**
ISBN 0-914667-10-6 $ 5.95

☐ **LIGHT FANTASTIC: Health-Conscious Entertaining by Janice Kenyon**
ISBN 0-9692194-3-1 $13.95

☐ **HAPPY BIRTHDAY: A Guide To Special Parties For Children by Smith & King**
ISBN 0-9610988-0-5 $ 9.95

☐ **CLASSIC LIQUEURS: The Art of Making & Cooking With Liqueurs by Long & Kibbey**
ISBN 0-914667-11-4 $ 8.95

☐ **EASY MICROWAVE PRESERVING by Fischborn & Long**
ISBN 0-914667-08-4 $10.95

☐ **WELCOME TO MICROWAVE LIVING: Micro-Convection Cooking by Susan Calder**
ISBN 0-919845-58-4 $13.95

☐ **WELCOME TO MICROWAVE COOKING by Susan Calder**
ISBN 0-9692008-0-3 $13.95

☐ **THE BEST OF SCANFEST edited by Cheryl Long**
ISBN 0-914667-13-0 $14.95

☐ **Please send a FREE complete catalog of books & specialty labels**

PLUS SHIPPING AND HANDLING $2.00

($3.00 FOR UPS)

Include a street address, not P.O. Box for UPS

Enclose check or
For Visa **VISA** or Mastercard **Master-Card** charge please complete:

Card # _____ Exp. Date: _____

Signature: _____

SHIP TO:

Name: _____
Address: _____
City/State: _____
Zip: _____ Area Code & Phone: _____

TO PROTECT BOOK, PLEASE PHOTOCOPY ORDERFORM.

*Our books are treasure-troves of information and ideas but
your satisfaction is priceless. Your comments are invited.*